7 Secrets to Successful Sales Management

The Sales Manager's Manual

7 Secrets to Successful Sales Management

The Sales Manager's Manual

Jack D. Wilner

S^t_L

St. Lucie Press

Boca Raton   London   New York   Washington, D.C.

Library of Congress Cataloging-in-Publication Data

Wilner, Jack D.
    7 Secrets to successful sales management : the sales manager's
manual / Jack D. Wilner.
        p. cm.
    Includes bibliographical references and index.
    ISBN 1-57444-088-8 (alk. paper)
    1. Sales management. I. Title.
HF5438.4.W536 1997
658.8'1—dc21   97-46631
                                                                CIP

© 1998 by CRC Press LLC
St. Lucie Press is an imprint of CRC Press LLC

No claim to original U.S. Government works
International Standard Book Number 1-57444-088-8
Library of Congress Card Number 97-46631
Printed in the United States of America   4 5 6 7 8 9 0
Printed on acid-free paper

Table of Contents

About the Author

Jack Wilner is a nationally recognized sales consultant and trainer with over 30 years of experience in sales and marketing. He received a B.S. degree from the U.S. Naval Academy and an M.B.A. from the Graduate School of Business, University of Chicago.

He is an active member of the American Society for Training and Development and is frequently selected as a speaker at the society's annual international conference. He is also a retired member of the Professional Society for Sales & Marketing Training, where he was recognized as a top-notch chairman of one of the society's best semiannual conferences on quality in sales.

Mr. Wilner has a solid background with Wrangler, one of the world's well-known jeans manufacturers. During his 20 years with Wrangler, he was a successful salesman and sales manager, prior to being promoted as Wrangler's first director of sales and marketing training. Since his retirement, he has become a results-oriented sales and marketing consultant and trainer in the U.S. as well as internationally. His clients include many Fortune 1000 companies in fields as diverse as apparel, automotive, communications, finance, food service, footwear, hardware, healthcare management, insurance, and retail, as well as a number of trade associations and professional societies.

A popular speaker at seminars and conferences around the world, Mr. Wilner has contributed to *Sales Management Handbook, Here Come the Sales Trainers,* and various sales journals. His wide assignment client base has provided him expertise in designing and delivering programs that are customized to the needs of the participants.

CHAPTER 1

The Sales Manager Looks Ahead

A quiet revolution is taking place in sales management, and you will want to be part of it. But in order to participate fully in the richness the future has to offer, you must realize that great changes are taking place.

This book is about what I have labeled the *seven secrets* a sales manager must master in order to succeed in the coming decades. Are they new or unique concepts? Not exactly. They are actually old ideas that must evolve with the times.

The Seven Secrets Will Sound Familiar

Vision, leadership, goal setting, recruitment, training, coaching, and motivation are all familiar terms. If you want to succeed as a sales manager in today's changing world, you must study these concepts carefully and make them part of your daily life. Today, more than ever before, these qualities and skills are critical to success in a sales management career.

This book is divided into two major parts. Part I is devoted to a detailed discussion of the "seven secrets" and how these general ideas relate to a successful sales management career. The information is designed to help you develop into the best sales manager you can be.

Part II contains additional practical material to help you implement— or *live*—the "seven secrets". Information and tips you can begin using today are provided on topics ranging from performance management to time management to managing meetings to developing strategic alliances.

Why, you might wonder, do sales managers need this information? There are many reasons, but the most important is that the future is not going to look like the past. Today's business leaders need different attitudes, skills, and knowledge in order to succeed. They need to be well-rounded individuals with a broad outlook and the ability to keep up with rapid change.

There are six areas that sales manager must be aware of in order to climb the stairway to success in this decade—and the next:

1. **Broadened responsibilities**—Former President Harry S. Truman had a sign on his Oval Office desk: "The Buck Stops Here". He left this as a legacy to us, and we must pick up the momentum, albeit 45 years later. The legacy is this: We are responsible for our actions. We must be more than salespeople, more than managers, more than trainers. We must be citizens and executives fully responsible for our actions and responsible to those with whom we do business, both internally and externally. On the corporate level, this is called *corporate social responsibility*; on the individual level, we shall call it *personal management responsibility.* If we want to earn good bucks, we must practice the Truman Doctrine: "The Buck Stops with Us".

2. **Team selling**—The old image of the salesperson as a rugged individualist is fading. Today's sales representative has become much more of a professional. The former one-man, backslapping, cigar-chomping powerhouse with his collection of whiz-bang jokes has gone the way of the cigar store Indian. As we move toward the year 2000, a highly coordinated and trained strategic sales team is taking over. Those who have not realized this must soon adjust to the new reality.

3. **Learning from the past**—Another well-known adage tells us that if we do not learn from history, we are condemned to relive it. In the professional sales field, we must learn from some of the "great ones" who have preceded us. Elmer Wheeler and his "sizzlemanship" became renowned around 1940. His classic selling words are still applicable. The Elmer Wheeler story is reviewed in Chapter 9. Another great professional, Dr. Ernest Dichter who became the "Father of Motivation", tells us what makes consumers tick and how we can market to them. The words of this giant will be discussed and analyzed in Chapter 8. Even the Willie Lomans will get their mention.

4. **Communication, cooperation, customer relations**—These "three C's" of modern salesmanship work together and can be the lubricant of sales success. Therefore, they are being incorporated in the modern sales manager's lexicon.

   Communication is the art of keeping in touch with all the groups that are necessary for the successful achievement of one's goals. These groups include one's own management, salespeople, suppliers, customers, marketers, and credit professionals. The art of communication has become so sophisticated that we no longer have any reason, other than our own incompetence, to ignore it.

   Cooperation is obvious and is expressed by the need for team selling.

   Customer relations involves the field of public relations and establishing a credible image for oneself, one's products and services, and the company or companies one represents.

5. **Outside–inside conflict resolution**—In order to concentrate sales and management efforts on the primary tasks—sales management and selling—we need to work in a smooth, pleasant, friction-free environment. Damaging interpersonal conflicts, whether within one's own staff and company or outside of them, need to be resolved quickly and completely. Profits are lost because of misunderstanding and distrust. There are few social or corporate situations that cannot be resolved by frank and open communication. Lose–lose situations will be discussed in some detail in this book because they are a cancer than can kill the patient.

6. **Team building**—In addition to team selling, it is vital to look at R&D. Strategic alliances also include outside groups such as suppliers, distributors, transporters, and local-level sellers. Secondary influences, such as government bodies and officials and the media, can also be included. Remember that alone we can fall, but together we can succeed. No goal is too great if we can all learn to work together. This is so important that Chapter 15 is devoted to strategic alliances.

Service, Service, Service

Sales management professionals can learn from real-estate professionals, as well as from the much touted Japanese management approach. Realtors say that three things make a property prime: location, location, location. In sales management today, as product differences are becoming less distinguishable, there are three reasons for the success of one product over another: service, service, service.

The Japanese approach to selling (some say it was an American who taught them the art) consists of a four-level process:

1. **Relationship selling**—This is the highest form of selling. Relationship selling is a way of building trust and cooperation that generates sales. It is not a theory; it is a process. In the introduction to his book *Relationship Selling, How to Get and Keep Customers,* Jim Cathcart says, "Relationship Selling transcends the sales transaction and looks beyond it to the ongoing relationship built between the buyer and the seller." Therefore, if you can't sell on the basis of relationship, then sell on the basis of value.

2. **Service selling**—Sell on the basis of service so that the customer knows that you have integrity, are credible, and are reliable. Then you can begin building trust and build confidence in your company, your product, and your service—as well as in you.

3. **Value selling**—Sell on the basis of the value your product and service offers that will satisfy the stated needs of your customer. If you can't sell on the basis of relationship or value, then sell on the basis of service.

4. **Price selling**—The lowest form of selling is based on price. While price is a factor, it is usually the last consideration.

Put these four steps together, and they spell RSVP. Practice them continually, and your customer will signal you: Respond, s'il vous plaît. Come again, please.

Problem Solving

Every business or profession has its pitfalls. One purpose of this book is to point out as many problems as possible and to offer case-by-case solutions to them. One semi-retired sales manager reflects on his lifetime of success by reiterating that you need to knock on ten doors before one will open to invite you in. This points out that one of the salesperson's greatest attributes is persistent customer contact. Few problems cannot be solved by persistent customer contact—by whatever manner or combination of ways is expedient and comfortable.

Some sales management problems can be solved by renewing the team's flagging motivation. Other problems can be remedied by such mundane things as realignment of territory and remuneration. Better time management, improved communication, using refreshing approaches such as the revival of humor, and continual coaching are all techniques to be remembered, renewed, and passed on.

In Price Pritchett's recent employee handbook, *New Work Habits for a Radically Changing World,* he says we should be fixers, not finger-pointers. Rather than trying to single out one of your sales staff to blame, assume ownership of problems. Let the solutions start with you. You'll increase your odds of success.

> We have only one person to blame, and that's each other.
>
> —Larry Beck, New York Ranger, on who started a brawl during the NHL's Stanley Cup playoffs.

Standards of sales performance require constant checking, coaching, reevaluation, and reinforcement. The steps that lead to superior standards of performance are making enough calls, expanding contacts with the decision makers, doing professional presentations, and using techniques of effective closing.

As we head at lightening speed toward a new millennium, it is important to remember that continuous education of our sales force is one of our most important requirements. Changes are taking place every day that affect sales management's prerogatives, responsibilities are increasing even as staffs are shrinking, and salespeople are being promoted into sales management and require new training and skills. We become coaches as well as managers. That's why coaching is one of the "seven secrets."

Learning to Spot New Opportunities

There are other important trends, some of which can be specifically defined. While it has long been known that age, gender, ethnicity, and so forth can affect sales and marketing programs, recognition of the diversity of markets is now *critical* to success. No matter what business you're in right now, be assured that what I call the "five E's" will figure in your sales and marketing programs. As we look forward to the beginning of an adventurous new millennium, keep these "five E's" in mind:

- Elderly customers
- Ethnic groups
- Environmental concerns
- Ethical revival
- Emphasis on quality

Some of these are known quantities, so to speak, but their importance can be easily underestimated. In fact, some people have never thought about the role of "five E's" in the future. To be successful today, however, sales managers must consider these issues. Let's look closely at each one and see what we can learn.

Elderly Customers

Targeting the more than 30 million active elderly Americans is a marketing "growth industry." To sell to them, you have to know them, especially if you are under 50.

Many elderly consumers have substantial discretionary income, but they are cautious in their spending. However, their income is quite level and fairly predictable. Half of America's discretionary income is held by seniors; 77 percent of U.S. household assets are in the hands of those over 50.

As sales professionals, we had better get to know the seniors' preferences—and they are not always what we assume. Seniors are merely grown-up juniors, and they carry many of their buying habits with them into their later years. Their loyalty to a brand is only marginally stronger than that of younger citizens. They respond to price promotions and special marketing incentives just as readily as younger buyers, perhaps even to a greater degree because seniors are often more frugal and are wise consumers.

Sometimes products have to be altered to accommodate needs of the elderly. Interior decorations, safety devices, lighting, medications, automobiles, travel services, and even sports equipment are all examples of products that are modified for older people. But don't keep reminding senior consumers of their age or frailties. They know the realities, but they don't want to be told about them at every turn. Instead, remind them that they have greater personal and financial freedom, that they deserve to treat themselves to better things, and that they are still responsive to romance and glamor.

There's money in the elderly market, and seniors are not afraid to spend it if you can punch the right key that opens the cash drawers.

The Ethnic Market

In addition to the elderly market, three major ethnic markets are growing steadily: the African-American market, the Hispanic market, and the Asian market. Projecting into the next decade, which is just around the bend, Hispanics are expected to grow to 11.1 percent of the U.S. population. By 2015, Hispanics are predicted to become the largest U.S. minority.

Another hot area for sales professionals is the Asian market. It is young, affluent, and well-educated. It is a highly quality-conscious group and growing fast. By the year 2000, it is expected to top 15 million, and by 2015, there might be 20 million Asian-Americans clamoring to join the consumer market.

Sales managers aiming at one or several of these ethnic markets must understand their diversity. Not all Asians are alike. There are 29 identifiable segments within the Asian-American community. An example of successful promotion to this market was conducted by the California State Lottery. It placed ads in domestic newspapers printed in Korean, Japanese, two Chinese dialects, Vietnamese, and Filipino.

Ask a Hispanic where he or she is from, and you won't hear Latin America or South America but rather the specific country, one of eight in Central America or one of a dozen in South America. Each has its own history, its own cuisine (and local restaurants), traditions, and dialectic variations. Promotions to this market segment are very specifically aimed at it, and by end of the next century, American business expects to invest as much as $60 billion in tapping the spending power of the nearly 30 million Hispanics in our midst.

In the same sense, the African-American market is not monolithic either. Each individual's roots are tied to some region within the U.S., a country in an area in Africa, or an island nation.

Environmental Concerns

Never underestimate the power of today's "green" consumers. They are concerned with the man-made hazards of our planet—with ways and means of correcting the correctable ones and with preventing further environmental abuses. They will support, even at a higher price, those companies that offer demonstrable "green" goods and services. They also applaud the real efforts that government agencies—national, state, and local—advance to keep our globe livable.

On a more practical level, not all environmental concerns are the province of the do-gooders or the alarmists. The environment has spawned many new businesses. Recycling, biodegradable products, services that prevent pollution, and goods made from recycled materials are all the result of catering to the "green" market. There are also costly industrial applications such as rustproof tanks, smokestack scrubbers, incineration plants, and replanting green spaces. These pursuits are creating vast new opportunities.

These environmental concerns and opportunities need to be stressed when training new salespeople and retraining older ones. If your product or service has any environmental advantages, highlight them. They could become potent sales tools in competent hands and measurable assets in competitive selling.

If you are convinced that environmental advantages could give your products a "leg up," you might even be able to persuade your company to consider them in its R&D and product development programs.

The last chapter in this book goes into greater detail on environmental, as well as ethical, considerations, not just as moral issues, but as pragmatic sales tools that will be used by tomorrow's sales force.

Ethical Revival

Ethical revival merits brief mention here (it is covered more thoroughly in Chapter 17). Business ethics is a very real force in our time. Despite abuses on Wall Street and in the backyards of some chemical plants, the hallways of legislatures, and the boardrooms of automotive giants, the United States is experiencing a certain moral regeneration. The pendulum is swinging, albeit slowly and slightly, toward a more humane way of doing business.

More than 200 colleges are teaching courses in business ethics. Even better, many companies, the small ones as well as the Dow Jones and Fortune 500 giants, are demonstrating that ethical policies affect their bottom lines in a positive manner. The public reacts favorably to companies and products and services that have ethical policies toward consumers, suppliers, governments, employees, and overseas trading partners.

Sales managers need to study this trend, to learn about the new emphasis on corporate social responsibility, and to help their companies lead in the thrust toward capitalism with a social conscience. The 21st century will see that such a policy is destined to pay off. A sales force that understands this policy will be better equipped to grow with its mentor, possibly its sales manager.

The following set of "commandments" serves as a wrap-up to this introductory discussion They are virtually Mosaic—a set of one dozen guidelines based on my past experience. They are every bit as relevant and adaptable today. I fervently believe that this advice is so basic to human nature that they will be equally useful in the coming millennium.

Advice to Managers Who Get the Good Jobs, Stay Employed, and Are Promoted

1. **Education** is a continuous effort. Today's world is changing too fast for anyone to graduate, and it takes no pity on the person who is lazy about learning. Besides, education is a genuine bargain. Only ignorance is expensive.

2. **Development** relates to the need to maintain a desire to improve your skills. Team building, not just individual excellence, is important, and teams are involved in decision making on every level and give attention to quality products and performance.

3. **That first impression** is important because you only have one opportunity to make a good first impression. First, pay attention to your appearance—dress the role. Make sure your shoes are polished to perfection. (Would you go to a dentist who has bad teeth?) Second, keep a positive, alert, and cheerful attitude. You don't like grumps, so don't be one.

4. **Stay cool** even when life at home, as well as at work, is full of stress. Work hard at controlling your temper. Teddy Roosevelt said, "Walk softly but carry a big stick." When you talk softly, you will probably be the only one who is heard—and remembered.

5. **Credibility** is a must for a product, a company reputation, and for the sales manager. If you establish a reputation for fairness and honesty, even occasional lapses will be forgiven. Such steadfast credibility is what makes good managers move upward.

6. **Visibility** in the right places and at the right time makes good managers better, especially when it comes to promotions. Your looks, your posture, your interaction, and your self-confidence all contribute. But be visible judiciously without being pushy.

7. **Management** of employees under you will make or break you. Hiring and retaining valuable people will enhance your position and make you look good. Give credit where credit is due—or you will create dangerous adversaries.

8. **Cooperation** with others is a sure step toward a promotion. Not all bread cast upon the waters comes back to feed you, but much of it does. While saying "yes" is not always feasible, remember that a "yes-person" goes a lot farther than a "no-person."

9. **Perseverance** to get a job done proves that you have the stuff to be a responsible manager and leader.

10. **Communication** is key to being understood by others. Speaking and writing clearly and correctly will enhance your reputation and get tasks done. Procrastination will leave tasks undone.

11. **Social skills** are a good manager's stock-in-trade. Doing the right thing at the right time—at holidays, at meetings, and at business gatherings—will establish your personality and reputation.

12. **Know how to blow your own horn** and know when and how loudly to blow it. Tactful aggressiveness and opportunism are real skills. If you know your business and think you're good, why hide your assets?

If you are convinced that the 1990s and beyond present new challenges and new opportunities, then begin—today—to adopt a new mindset, one based on the "seven secrets." You, the company you work for, and your sales staff will benefit from your efforts.

It all starts with vision, so let's explore this large, but sometimes elusive, concept.

Part I

The Seven Secrets

CHAPTER 2

Secret #1: Vision

Sales managers who have vision can predict the future—simply because they create it! Vision is innovating a *purposeful, organized* search for change. It is not for the timid. Vision has elements of invention, entrepreneurship, curiosity, and adventure. The sales manager whose focus is on next Friday's paycheck is obviously not a visionary.

There is, no doubt, an element of risk in being a visionary. Not every corporation welcomes a visionary, and not every visionary fits into a corporate mold. However, those who are fortunate enough to be a member of a visionary company know that there is no limit to achievement. Sales managers with vision have no horizons, and the corporation that shares such vision does not stand in the way on the rainbow road to that glorious pot of gold.

What are the secrets of sales mangers with vision? They are long-term oriented. They can look five to ten years into the future as clearly as the narrow-minded can see to the ends of their noses. On the pragmatic side, visionary sales managers are able to assure themselves with an incentive-based contract that pegs remuneration to imagination.

Who Are Some People with Vision?

Visionaries are legion in American business. We are fortunate to be able to draw on a treasure of examples. A century ago, R.H. Macy saw that a square block of stores under one roof could become the world's mightiest retail enterprise—and so it happened.

In the rough-and-tumble 1930s, retailers used to say "look at Macy's" when they faced a problem. Of course, Macy's has since had its share of problems, and perhaps the visionary light that was furnished by its founder has dimmed.

Ray Kroc is another visionary who saw in a small West Coast hamburger stand the beginning of a world empire selling billions of Big Macs. For tens of thousands of employees and franchisees, he created his "McMotto: Quality, Service, Cleanliness, Value."

Billionaire Sam Walton, a small-town boy from Bentonville, Arkansas and founder of Wal-Mart, had a vision that led to one of the world's most profitable and ubiquitous retail operations. His vision is capsulized in a four-point maxim:

1. Be friendly to customers
2. Be tough to suppliers
3. Be inspirational to employees
4. Be extremely profitable to shareholders

Note that these examples illustrate people who could see a decade or more ahead. They never lost sight of their goals, and they were able to make their vision pragmatic with the right means that led to their envisioned ends.

The following story exemplifies the heights to which a person with vision can rise. Three brick masons were working side by side when a passerby stopped to admire their handiwork.

> "What are you doing?" inquired the onlooker.
>
> "Laying bricks," replied the first mason. "What does it look like?"
>
> Not taken aback, the bypasser asked the second mason, "And what are you doing?"
>
> "I am building a wall," answered the second mason, just a little impatiently.
>
> "And what about you?" The pedestrian asked the last mason. "What are you doing?"
>
> The third man straightened himself up, looked the inquirer in the eyes, and replied, "Me? I'm building a handsome mansion!"

One man out of three was able to see past the brick and mortar and was able to envision the glorious results of their labor. He was able to transform the ordinary into an extraordinary vision. Chances are that man will be the supervisor next year, or maybe the general contractor.

Planning versus Vision

A generation ago, organizations talked about management by objectives, and then along came strategic planning. Both methods relied heavily—and still do—on facts, figures, and top management opinions, hardly the stuff that engenders enthusiasm from employees and the kind of motivation that will show up in a commission check or on the bottom line.

True leaders, however, discovered *vision.* Henry Ford had it, and his pal Thomas Alva Edison had it, too. Many leaders have it today, and their names have become well-known in many industries and professions.

The United States had Thomas Paine, Thomas Jefferson, and Benjamin Franklin and later Abraham Lincoln and Franklin Roosevelt. Latin America had Simon Bolivar, and Italy had Garibaldi. They were all visionaries who measured time not in days or months, but in years and decades.

Real leaders, whether in sales, management, marketing, or production, also have that often indefinable extra called *vision.* Perhaps they can see something ordinary mortals can't, but vision can be enhanced, dramatized, verbalized—and perhaps even taught.

Superior sales performance can also be envisioned. It is expressed in terms of creating mental pictures, visions that capture the imagination, and in developing increased employee performance along the way. By allowing employees the freedom to draw on their own talents and initiatives, you might unlock a treasure of performance that will surprise both the performer and the supervisor.

The Visioning Experience

At the top echelons of business, there are visionary companies like Disney, 3M, Motorola, Hewlett-Packard, Boeing, MCI, Wrangler, and Ben & Jerry's Ice Cream. All of these companies, and hundreds more, have certain similarities which, when examined analytically, reveal their secrets of success—and they all start with a clear vision of where they are going.

To make visioning a positive experience and apply it to your situation, bear in mind the following principles:

- **It's a slow process**—Visioning is a slow process, like aging a great wine. It will probably take a year to focus on your vision and a decade to implement it. It is long range, not short range.

- **It's everyone's property**—Visioning is the property of the leader and all the people who implement the leader's vision. It has to come from deep within the company and include every employee who shares the leader's commitment and shares his or her sense of ownership.

- **It requires patience**—Visioning cannot be crammed down the throats of those who fail to understand the leader's vision. Be patient in convincing them that their deeper analysis, planning, and goals will be respected and incorporated in the general scheme of the visioning process.

- **It requires timing and commitment**—Visioning requires exquisite timing. It can only work if the leader is convinced and wholeheartedly committed to the vision. A vision cannot grow in infertile or bitter soil or when other problems (lawsuits, disastrous competition, financial fiasco, etc.) burden corporate leadership.

As a general principle of making visions come true, remember that even with superior sales management, effective visions must flow from deep within the organization. They must percolate upward from the inside out, not from the top down. A vision might start with one person, but it becomes reality only when all get behind it—*e pluribus unum.*

The Importance of Personal Vision

If you are looking for salespeople who share your vision, why not ask them? Most probably won't qualify, but you just might discover that gem who will dovetail with your vision of where you want to go—and you will have forged a symbiosis that can pay off for many years to come.

Bonnie St. John Deane had the vision to succeed, despite every handicap imaginable. She was an amputee, the child of a single mother, black— and immensely successful. She was a medalist in the U.S. Olympics for the Disabled, in skiing no less, and an important worker in the Clinton White House, where she was asked to coordinate a task force on training. It was only natural that she approach department heads whose titles promised great responses. She discovered, to her consternation, that these high-powered officials were unable to offer any constructive help. Their personal vision was mostly political or self-motivated. Bonnie Deane said she learned a lesson from this experience: "I confused their job titles with their personal interests."

Her lesson can be valuable for sales managers: Sales team leaders need to harnass their salespeople's personal visions in order to get the most from the sales team. Therefore, if you have a personal vision of your company's goals, articulate that dream and share it with others, in order to make it real. If you then can find others who see that vision clearly and will act upon it, you've got an unbeatable team.

Keep in mind that today's visionary will be tomorrow's leader, which is the "secret" revealed in the next chapter.

> Make your vision as clear as your profit goals. Profit alone is not enough to motivate your people. Expand the scope of your vision to address more of the whole person.
>
> —Joseph Quigley
> *Vision, How Leaders Develop It, Share It, and Customize It*

CHAPTER 3

Secret #2: Leadership

Managers are bottom-line oriented. They work along reasonably established and secure lines. It is their job to train people, not to educate them. Leaders are the conductors; they rise to the top despite possible weaknesses. Warren Bennis, author of *On Becoming a Leader* and other books, articulated a dozen excellent principles that dramatize the differences between managers and leaders:

- The manager administers; the leader innovates.
- The manager is a copy; the leader is an original.
- The manager maintains; the leader develops.
- The manager focuses on systems and structures; the leader focuses on people.
- The manager relies on control; the leader inspires trust.
- The manager has a short-range view; the leader has a long-range perspective.
- The manager asks how and when; the leader asks what and why.
- The manager has his eye always on the bottom line; the leader has his eye on the horizon.
- The manager imitates; the leader originates.
- The manager accepts the status quo; the leader challenges it.
- The manager is the classic good soldier; the leader is his own person.
- The manager does things right; the leader does the right things.

If you are a sales manager who is looking ahead, Bennis's principles may inspire you.

Learning to Be a Leader

After interviewing dozens of leaders in American business, Bennis, who is a professor of management at the University of Southern California, described the following four major strengths that make these men and women successful beyond their peers:

1. Attention through vision
2. The means to communicate vision
3. Positive self-regard
4. Ability to build trust with their associates

"Vision—dreams—creates attention and draws others to it," Bennis says. "Many leaders are passionate dreamers. They have deeply felt convictions about what they want to achieve. Successful leaders have learned to communicate their visions to others and inspire participation."

Leaders of all types know that they have to rationally and logically convince others that their vision is just and proper. The right response from their followers has to come out of conviction, not force.

How can leaders communicate their vision? "Many leaders are very articulate," says Dr. Bennis. Some have found "unusual non-verbal ways to communicate." They will use established images that can be seen, felt, and touched in order to bring their subordinates and co-workers to believe in their vision.

The self-image of leaders is not an ego trip. They are fully aware of their capabilities and have the confidence to share their power and knowledge. "Leaders look upon mistakes as learning experiences," states Warren Bennis. He relates an anecdote from the files of IBM to illustrate.

It seems that a young executive, involved in an IBM venture that turned sour, offered his resignation to then-chairman Tom Watson, Jr. The great IBM executive looked at the contrite manager and said, "You can't be serious. We can't accept your resignation. After all, IBM just spent $10 million educating you!"

Building trust with colleagues comes from the leader's own experiences. The leader has watched others succeed as well as fail and has learned from others and listened to them. Bennis says that "accepting candid feedback from trusted colleagues" is one of the leader's major assets.

"The experiences of many of our country's top leaders have convinced me that leadership skills can be learned," explains Bennis.

Leaders Are Not Born, They Are Made

Everyone has leadership potential. "The most common trait shared by successful leaders is a positive self-image," says Dr. Geri McArdle, a Reston, Virginia, trainer and writer.

Studies have shown that earlier achievements, or the lack of them, are *not* indicative of future successes. Think back to your own high-school classmates, and you will probably arrive at the same conclusion. The kids in your class who made straight As were the best looking, were the most active, were the best connected in local society, or were just plain lucky were not necessarily the ones who became leaders later in life.

My own experience in a small-town group bears this out. One of the poorest boys in class became a prominent and very wealthy surgeon—the only one in the group to achieve this status. The class country bumpkin, handicapped by both looks and assumed low intellect, became a successful local merchant and owner of two buildings and a huge inventory of merchandise, all fully paid for.

Dr. McArdle suggests that you ask yourself six questions in order to get to know yourself better and determine if you have leadership potential:

1. **Do I have the discipline and dedication to keep going and avoid being side-tracked?** In other words—do you have the ability to keep your eye on the ball at all times?

2. **Do I have the energy to give the extra time and care required?** Caring does not take extra time; carelessness does.

3. **Am I resourceful and flexible?** The world is full of obstacles; some people are stopped by them, and others see them as opportunities. Few things in life are entirely black or white; sometimes you have to go with the gray.

4. **Can I enjoy myself making the best of every situation?** Great sales don't happen; we *make* them happen. If you are philosophical about life, you can cope with whatever comes along.

5. **Do I have the necessary competence or will I be able to learn fast?** Having the desire, the motivation, the focus toward a rational goal will make you competent. Keeping your eyes and ears, but especially your mind, open will help you learn. Don't be impatient; learning is a lifetime job.

6. **The strength of your personal vision can help you build a powerful, compelling personality. Do I have that vision?** Only you can answer that question, because leadership comes from within.

As Dr. McArdle says, "Successful leaders are certain about where they want to go in life and about their positive self-image; they make sure they get there." Do not look to the outside for your solutions to the leadership puzzle; look inside. Get to know *yourself* better.

> Who should be Sales *Manager*? That is like asking, who should sing tenor in the church choir? Obviously the person who can sing tenor.
>
> —(after) Henry Ford

> Behind an able manager, are always other able men.
>
> —Chinese proverb

> The manager administers, the leader innovates. The manager maintains, the leader develops. The manager relies on systems, the leader relies on people. The manager counts on controls, the leader counts on trust. The manager does things right, the leader does the right things.
>
> —*Fortune* magazine

> In simplest terms, a leader is one who knows where he wants to go, gets up, and goes.
>
> —John Erskine

> Eagles don't flock—you have to find them one at a time.
>
> —H. Ross Perot

> We can't all be heroes. Somebody has to sit on the curb and clap as they go by.
>
> —Will Rogers

Training for Leadership

Managers obviously have to manage one or more people. Leadership imposes the duty to train others in the way you and your company wants to do business. The men and women who work produce results. This also makes you responsible for the behavior and results of those who have been put in your charge. You get to inherit the glory—and the responsibility.

One of your responsibilities as a leader will be to develop a training system. This system includes visual components such as posters, videos, 35mm slides, overhead transparencies, role modeling, tricks, devices, and a lot of pop psychology. Like a motivational speaker at a sales and training seminar or a charismatic television preacher, you will want to whip up enthusiasm from your audience.

As a leader, your training programs will generally fall into three categories:

1. **Expertise**—Instilling the proper expertise or technical skills your trainees need to perform professionally. While your trainees might already possess these skills, they will still need to adjust them to conform with your way of doing things—your leadership—and with the goals of your company.

2. **Motivation**—This is the second phase. (Chapter 8 is devoted to this topic because it is an important "secret.") Motivation is a training technique; it is part of psychology and flowered in the post-World War II years. If your trainees are really *sold* on your product or service, they will produce better results, for both you and themselves. Whether you call it willingness, enthusiasm, desire, hunger, or esprit de corps, it all boils down to motivation.

3. **Value or benefits**—The third training step is to demonstrate the value or benefits of your product or service to ultimate customers—the *results* the trainee will personally derive from doing a good job. Everyone on every level looks for personal benefits—for himself or herself, for family, company, group, or country. Results are what everybody works for. It's the sizzling bacon that will stimulate success.

Nothing stimulates training like being enthusiastic and *positive*. This word can be used to illustrate a series of training and leadership principles:

Planning
Organizing
Stimulating/stretching your efforts
Information seeking
Time management
Idea creation
Value promotion
Efficiency

When your sales staff does well, *you* will look good. When they are well-trained, display expertise, are motivated, and are confident that their achievements will be rewarded, they will be happier, stay longer, and produce more.

Professional trainers, who are by definition leaders, have evolved a series of benefits that appropriate training will bring the trainee:

- Helps the employee make better decisions and solve problems effectively
- Instills motivation that can lead to recognition, achievement, growth, responsibility, and advancement
- Aids in encouraging and achieving self-development and self-confidence
- Helps an employee handle tension, stress, frustration, and conflict
- Provides information for improving leadership knowledge, communication skills, and attitudes
- Increases job satisfaction
- Moves the employee toward personal goals while improving interpersonal skills
- Satisfies goals and needs of both trainer and trainee
- Provides trainee with an avenue for growth and a say in his or her future
- Helps develop speaking and listening skills and, if they are part of the training process, writing skills, too
- Helps to reduce fears encountered by trainees when confronted with new tasks

The organization will also benefit from such a leadership training program because it will create a better working environment. Here is a working list of 17 ways your company can benefit:

- Fosters more positive attitudes toward company goals
- Leads to greater profitability for both company and salesperson
- Improves morale of work force
- Helps to create a better corporate image
- Improves attitudes between bosses and employees
- Transmits a more positive company image to the outside world
- Aids in team development
- Helps to prepare guidelines for work
- Establishes a conduit from which the company can learn from the employees
- Establishes a framework for promotions from within
- Aids in developing leadership qualities, motivation, loyalty, better attitudes, and other aspects of management–worker relations
- Can reduce outside consulting costs by using internal skills
- Stimulates preventative management, rather than settling problems after they have become public
- Reduces internal theft and behavior that reduces efficiency
- Creates an appropriate climate for growth and communication
- Helps employees, both old and new, adjust to corporate changes and new policies
- Helps to prevent conflict and stress by providing a tool for reducing tension

The bottom line of all of these efforts is that your company's profit-and-loss statement will reflect all your efforts, and *you* are the key player.

Leaders Work Smarter, Not Harder

When you were a kid, you may have bought one of those contraptions called Chinese handcuffs. You put your index fingers into each end of the little woven straw tube. If you pulled your fingers to get them out of the tube, it didn't work. The more frantically you pulled, the tighter the tube grabbed your fingers. After an initial moment of panic, you found that if you relaxed and pushed your fingers rather than pulling them, the straw tube would ease up and allow your fingers to be withdrawn.

Perhaps there is a lesson to be learned here: *Think* your way out of tough situations; don't fight your way out. Working smarter, not harder, will produce greater results, and you'll have plenty of energy left over to fight another battle.

The "Societal Disease" of Our Time

"Corporate ethical decline is the direct result of our bottom-line mentality," said Norman Lear, mentor of modern television and producer of many programs, including *All in the Family.* "I think that's where the greatest impact on our culture might have been, in other times, the church, education, the family. The greatest impact now is *business.* Everywhere one looks, it seems to me that short-term thinking in business has great impact on our culture. And that's *leadership,* because it's certainly educating kids to believe there's nothing between winning and losing...Short-term thinking is the societal disease of our time."

The Next Generation of Leaders

Our upcoming leaders will have some characteristics in common. Look for these qualities in the people you choose to take your company into the third millennium:

- Belief in people and teamwork
- Boundless curiosity about the world around them
- Broad education rather than "premature" specialists
- Commitment to excellence
- Enthusiasm galore
- Innovative, willing to try new venues
- Readiness to tackle new tasks
- Orientation to long-term growth rather than short-term goals

- Accept ethics and environmental concerns as partners in future planning
- Vision to see beyond the immediate horizon
- Willingness to take calculated risks

The Secrets of Effective People and Companies

Success is totally neutral. It does not discriminate against age, gender, race, political belief, or religion. Yet there are steps that successful executives, including sales managers and their companies, have taken that make them stand out from the crowd. Fortunately, success, like leadership, can be studied. It is not like your grandmother's private recipes or a closely guarded trade secret.

One of the first criteria we note is that the majority of new, fast-track companies are *team efforts.* Their leaders are not solitary solos reposing on their own Mount Olympus or in an ivory tower communicating with the muses. Most of the visible successes are *partnerships.*

In a study of midwestern companies that had substantial track records, 6 percent were founded by a single entrepreneur, 54 percent were started by a two-person partnership, and 40 percent had three or more founders. The same study surveyed slow- or low-growth companies and discovered that 42 percent of them were solo ventures, 43 percent were partnerships (two persons), and 15 percent had three or more founders.

The team concept is also noted in other operational areas. Of the 500 most successful companies reported in an *INC. 500* list, half shared private fiscal information with their employees (traditionally, this information is private), 33 percent had formal boards of directors, and another 33 percent had created informal advisory panels.

Sales managers can take advantage of these findings. Leadership is not always a solitary occupation, but rather a way of working together as a team with everyone responsible for a company's success. Teamwork gives companies a better chance to survive and thrive.

Successful managers *know their business. INC.* magazine's recent list of companies showed that the leaders of these companies had ten or more years of experience in the same industries in which they later started businesses. The contrast with the slow- or no-growth companies was dramatically evident: Most of their leading executives were relatively new to their companies or had limited experience in their fields. They had evidently started their businesses with more hope and intuition than pragmatic knowledge.

The new fast-track executives often came from larger companies that had squeezed them out in the wake of mergers and downsizing. In the 1980s, only 6 to 8 percent of start-ups were headed by former large company executives; by the early 1990s, this had grown to 20 percent. These numbers show that experience counts.

This emergence of former managers-turned-entrepreneurs leads to an additional conclusion: These new stars were used to operating at a corporate level and were accustomed to working with others. Ergo, they applied proven methods to their operations and used teamwork in their own fast-growth enterprises.

> The more you *know,*
> the faster you can *GO!*

Successful people are *multitalented* and highly *experienced,* but entrepreneurs are not born, they are made. Of a large group of successful managers, only 20 percent went into business and survived.

A far larger group, 63 percent, had started at least one other business and either left it, sold it, or it failed before they became successful in their current enterprise. In fact, another 17 percent had started three or more businesses in their careers.

There is a downside to these statistics. When a successful entrepreneur leaves a business, it often becomes a victim of an entrepreneurial disease—bankruptcy. The cause may not be immediately apparent and may fester for some time. Perhaps mismanagement or a lack of enthusiastic management of the founder is to blame. In a survey among a group of 343 businesses that were sold by their successful founders, only 27 percent were still in existence a few years later. All progress involves risk, but knowledge minimizes it.

Financing is thought to be one of this successful group of companies' major assets, but as Duke Ellington said in his song, "It ain't necessarily so." While the surveys of successful companies indicated a slight fiscal superiority, money without management expertise does not alone guarantee success.

The U.S. Census Bureau found that all start-up companies started with somewhat less than ideal capitalization. Thirty percent began with less than $5,000. In fact, of the 500 most successful enterprises checked by

INC. magazine in 1992, a full 22 percent managed to get off the ground with less than $5,000 and still grew into the top success category. To be realistic, about one-third of start-up companies began with $50,000 or more, and 50 percent among the above *INC.* group were launched with at least that much, while only 7 percent began with a million dollars or more.

> Money is often a lubricant, but does not move the engine.
> Only good leadership and management can do that.

Those companies that require more start-up money are usually manufacturers or research and development companies, where steady cash flow and profits often happen well in the future. Very few of the companies surveyed, none among the fastest growing ones, were financed by venture capital.

Multiple ownership has been found to be a boon to burgeoning businesses. Diverse talents add to the success and survival of new companies; autocratic, inbred ownership and management, so popular several generations ago, appears to be a brake on success.

Ownership is usually defined by the amount of money invested by the entrepreneur. Among the success leaders, about half owned 50 percent of their companies; 29 percent did not invest any of their own money in their operations. The U.S. Census Bureau reveals that half of the best companies raised no equity capital whatsoever, relying solely on the founders' private money.

The moral of this story is that successful entrepreneurs accumulate considerable capital before they get started, have good money-raising track records (which by inference means that they have sterling reputations), and have a pronounced team orientation. In other words, they do not mind sharing the ownership of their companies, knowing that such diversity of responsibilities and skills can only benefit their enterprises. In short, they know that *leaders* always work with others.

> No matter how smart you are, as often as not,
> two heads are better than one.

Taking a broad and even global viewpoint in marketing products and services was one of the major hallmarks of all successful companies checked. The U.S. Department of Commerce conducted a study among young fast-track companies which confirmed this.

The really hot companies of the 1990s are those that include international trading and regional selling in their marketing plans. In fact, as much as 40 percent of all U.S. products and services sold outside of the U.S. come from the top 10 percent of small businesses. This realization should give wings to support for small and new businesses by government agencies, banks, and financiers.

Establishing relations with larger companies, known as strategic alliances, is also one of the tools smart small companies use. One third of the bright high-growth companies have such relationships with larger corporations and, as a result, have expanded their marketing territories and revenues well beyond those achieved by companies that tried to grow alone. It appears, then, that cooperation, collaboration, sharing, and a non-parochial view are the stepping-stones to business success.

To operate successfully in the highly complex 21st century marketplace, profitable companies must be a part of the greater fabric of our globe. They need knowledge, understanding, and, as discussed in Chapter 2, vision.

> A good leader knows how to get the best
> from his or her employees by listening.

Sources of Employee Stress

Seven major gripes reduce employee effectiveness. Good leaders will try to avoid or remedy them.

	Sources of job stress
Fear of job loss	47 percent
Unnecessary paperwork	42
Bosses who don't listen	37
Meetings that are time-wasters	31
Destructive, unconfirmed rumors	17
No attainable goals	12
Voice or e-mail to avoid contact	8

While we like to be positive, there are times when it helps to know what *not* to do. Here is a checklist of "don'ts." You might agree or disagree with them—it depends on your own personality and style of management—but consider them anyway, just to be sure:

- **Don't be negative**—Don't tell your staff what they did wrong; instruct them about how to do it right.

- **Don't cover up mistakes**—Encourage people to report mistakes so everyone can learn from them.

- **Don't dwell on mistakes**—Errors are opportunities for improvement and growth.

- **Don't make unfair comparisons**—Compare a salesperson's performance with his or her previous record, not with another person's.

- **Don't suffer from I-strain**—Learn to listen as well as give advice. Clear understanding is inevitably followed by positive action.

- **Don't manage without a plan of action**—To get optimum results, your plan should include:
    a. Goals
    b. Clear communication
    c. Accountability
    d. Follow-up

A Few Nuggets to Mine from the Minds of America's Best Sales Managers

- **Case histories**—These are wonderful tools, and some colleges use them like the Ten Commandments. But they need to be considered for what they are—the experiences of individuals and companies and not always applicable as is to your needs.

- **Ask questions**—The best way to learn is to ask questions. The answers can often fill in the gaps in your own knowledge, and others will feel important and flattered that you sought their advice.

- **Network**—Since no man is an island, make use of the world around you. Co-workers, customers, suppliers, the trade media, volunteer organizations, and professional and civic associations all contribute to your expertise as an effective sales manager.

- **Education**—Whatever your profession, business, or ambition, education is a lifetime job. Attend workshops and seminars, read trade and professional publications, study audiotape programs, attend lectures, and talk with your peers at pertinent gatherings. Whatever the price, it's a bargain when compared to the cost of ignorance.

- **Building long-term relationships**—Just as Rome was not built in a day, so building relationships with customers and clients is not a one-shot job. Patience, time, genuine information, and understanding human motivation and benefits interact to make sales and satisfaction. Keeping a customer happy over a period of time builds credibility and confidence which even competition and reverses will have a hard time knocking down.

- **Build trust**—Whether you call it trust or credibility, it works not only in day-to-day selling but especially in times of trouble and turmoil. Sam Walton was a genius at this and built a multibillion-dollar empire on selling trust. Offer honest value and honest advice; make business ethics a partner in your progress. It's the bread cast upon the water that will always come back to feed you when the going gets tough. Besides, you'll probably sleep better.

Go back to the list of qualities that leaders possess; post the list in your office or home. And always remember that leadership will be a secret to your success.

> Success is not a goal. Success is a result.
>
> —Don Beveridge

CHAPTER 4

Secret #3: Goals—You Must Have Them

> Your Company is not in the tourist business. Without a call
> objective a sales rep is merely a well-paid tourist.
>
> —Jack Falvey

Hal Wright, a small-business consultant and author of *How to Make 1000 Mistakes in Business and Still Succeed,* tells the story of a business owner who came to him for help. She told him how much (actually how little) money she made the previous year. In a friendly tone, Hal asked her how much money she had planned to make. She responded in a puzzled voice, saying that she really hadn't planned her income. Hal then said, "Gosh, since you didn't really plan to make any money, you really did better than you thought you would."

Hal's story perfectly illustrates the importance of setting goals and forming plans to reach those goals. As Hal puts it: "You'll never accomplish much more than you plan to accomplish." Hal Wright calls this a rule of thumb, and it is one his clients never forget—or they simply don't continue working with him.

Goal setting is one of the most important keys to a sales manager's success. Furthermore, it is the next step after forming a vision. The goals should reflect the vision, and as a manager, you are in a position to pass this wisdom on to those who work for you. In fact, by setting goals and making plans to reach them, you are functioning as a role model. What kind of role model would you like to be?

Hey, I've Got Goals—In My Head!

If you consider your future important enough to plan for, then I suggest that you write your goals down. Hal Wright believes that unwritten goals tend to be forgotten, and people who don't bother to clearly state their goals in writing are usually not taking the goals very seriously. Goals held only in our own minds are generally more like vague dreams.

Ask any successful person, and you will find that he or she has goals, takes those goals seriously, and frequently engages in a process of evaluating and up-dating them. Why not tell this to your sales staff? See if it motivates them into action.

Goal Setting Is Motivating

> No one ever accomplishes anything of consequence without a goal...Goal setting is the strongest human force for self-motivation.
>
> —Paul Myer

There is no question that motivation is crucial. But if we don't have goals, what are we motivated about? Enthusiasm is great, but when we describe people as enthusiastic, we can usually say that they are directing their energy toward something. As often as not, that something is a goal or an objective that is part of a long-term goal.

Specific objectives are as important as the larger concept of goals. Objectives can be viewed as small goals that must be reached before a larger goal can be attained.

- Objectives specify a direction to take toward reaching a specific target.
- Objectives state what will happen to a specific part of the business, how much will happen, and by when it will happen.

Suppose your goal is to increase sales by 15 percent over the previous year. You might outline specific sales objectives for each month. On a personal level, your goal might be to save $5,000 for a trip to South America. You determine that it will take 24 months to reach your goal, and you begin planning for the four-week trip. Because your income fluctuates seasonally, you state your month-to-month savings objectives based on your projected income. (This goal could be part of a bigger picture. Maybe your goal is to learn all you can about the rain forests throughout the world, and this trip will be your first step toward reaching your goal.)

Your savings goal for your trip has the five essential characteristics of setting effective goals and objectives. When training your sales staff about goals, use the following acronym to help them remember each important element:

Specific
Measurable
Attainable
Realistic
Time-bound

Let's take a look at how SMART works in sales—and in life.

Specific—This simply means focusing on the objective and not meandering and perhaps losing both the ball game and the customer. It means describing in minute detail the actual sales work necessary to execute a sales strategy. Suppose your goal is to increase the number of sales calls per week. If you say you will make 12 calls per week and that's two more than previously scheduled, then that's a specific objective.

Measurable—Have you ever had a goal that was really more like a dream? Most of us have. We might say, "I'd like to be more *successful* or *happier* or *financially secure.*" These may sound good, but what do they mean? They lack specificity as described above. How would you know if you attained them? What does success look like? What is it going to take for you to be happier? What amount of money will make you feel financially secure? Can you outline what security would look and feel like?

One reason so few people very seriously plan and execute their goals is because they are too imprecise. No wonder so much goal setting is abandoned. If, however, we decide to state our goals in such a way that we can measure progress, then we have specific targets. Eliminate "approximately" or "about." What counts is the tangible result. If we decide to increase sales calls per week from 10 to 12, then we can measure how well we're doing. If we make 11 calls, we've fallen short by one. If we make 13 the next week, then we've evened the total.

Attainable—Can the goal be reached or are we setting ourselves up to fail? One problem with vague, non-specific, non-measurable goals is that they are generally not attainable. What if I said I wanted to become an opera singer by next summer, but I've never had a voice lesson and I can't carry a tune? Is that an attainable goal? Probably not. It's amazing how many people call a passing dream a goal, which generally prevents them from getting down to the serious—but satisfying—business of forming attainable goals.

Attainable goals are matched with knowledge, desire, ambition, attitude, and talent. Your staff must have the desire to increase the number of sales calls made and must know how they can do it. How many more cold calls will it require? Where will the leads come from? The answers to these questions lead to the next element.

Realistic—A goal is realistic if it falls into the category of the concrete— working with situations and conditions the way they actually are instead of the way we might dream they ought to be. In the sales setting, realistic expectations would include:

- Your company's mission and objectives
- Your customers' objectives and needs
- Your actual internal and external resources available
- Your relationships with others, including personalities, compatibility, and conflicts
- Your own perception of what you believe can be achieved, devoid of any pie-in-the-sky illusions
- The economic conditions surrounding customers that affect their buying decisions

The concept of realism in your goals will vary throughout your career. Times change, abilities and skills are added, economic forecasts rise and fall, and unexpected events happen. Sometimes people fail to set goals because they are afraid that conditions will change. They are right— things change—which makes it all the more important to set goals. Goals are the anchor that keeps us steady in fluctuating times. We must adapt as times change. The manufacturers of slide rules had to set new goals when calculators made their product obsolete. In 1990, increasing slide rule sales would be an unrealistic goal indeed, but in 1950, it was a sound goal based on facts available at that time.

Time-bound—Like may things in life, goals must have a beginning, a middle, and an end. The best goals can fit neatly into a time frame, and generally, short term is best. Doubling sales in six months during a recession may not be a realistic goal, depending on the product, of course. Doubling sales in two years could be a realistic goal, which offers time segments in which to measure target objectives along the way. It is also important to allow some leeway, or you may be too hard on yourself. Generally speaking, there is no objective that cannot be achieved; if an objective is not achieved, the reason is usually an unrealistic time frame.

A goal is nothing more than a dream with a time limit.

—Joe L. Griffith

Applying SMART to Sales

Before you can score you must first have a goal.

—Anonymous

The methods used to develop a winning sports team are not unlike those used to build a winning sales team. You have to set a realistic, attainable objective. Let's say that your team has a current batting average of .272, but you think that a 25 percent increase is achievable. This translates into elevating your team from .272 to .340, which is probably unrealistic. However, a 10 percent increase could be both realistic and achievable, and the team can wind up batting a respectable .300.

Let's say you want to achieve a 10 percent increase in sales. Your own experience tells you that, on average, your sales staff must make at least five prospect calls to get one positive result (an order or an indication of serious interest).

Your sales team's customer list includes 100 companies that buy products from your company at least once a year. You need 10 more customers, and your sales team must make 50 sales calls on prospective buyers. That breaks down to only one extra sales call by one of your sales staff per week, or two salespeople making one extra call per week over a six-month period. Of course, you could also apply this to expanding your business with existing customers.

People who know where they are going know how to get there. In football, it may be a short pass to gain five yards and then one or two running plays to make a first down, or it could be a long pass into the end zone for a touchdown. Business is similar. The extra sales calls are like running plays to achieve a first down and then on to a touchdown. When Steve Jobs, founder of Apple Computer, was 12 years old, he called Bill Hewlett, founder of Hewlett-Packard, and asked if he would give him some parts.

Alone or Part of the Team

Once you have set specific goals for your team, don't be discouraged if your goals don't coincide exactly with each individual's goal. Perhaps you need to adjust the team's goals. Get the sales team together to brainstorm and reach *congruency,* so that you will all be operating on the same wavelength again.

Sales staff *confidence* increases as individuals reach their own goals and see the team's goals being reached because of their success. Each achievable plateau builds more confidence, which allows for even more growth.

Remember, too, that goals must be *customized* for each salesperson. What Mary can achieve might not be possible for Angela, who just started a sales career. While Joe might be a star salesperson, his peer, Mark, might never be a star. This could be because he lacks strong drive and ambition, or it could be the result of lesser natural or inborn ability. Where Joe finds it easy to reach his goals, Mark must work harder and struggle. (This is why we have—and will always have—A, B, and C salespeople.)

Use your experience and a dose of psychology to sell your goals to your team. There are bound to be those who won't reach them. After all, not everybody can be first on a sales team, any more than all 25 players on a baseball team can have the same batting average.

If you decide to keep the laggerds on staff and want to spur them on to greater goals next month, assure those individuals that failure is not the end of the world and that they can learn from non-successes. Fear of failure can be paralyzing, freezing sales staff into inaction.

In tennis, golf, and kicking extra points in football, *follow-through* is essential for success. In sales, follow-through is essential, too. It is smart to follow-through on your sales plans and let your sales team know that you are keeping statistical analyses based on their reports. This is as smart in sales as it is in sports.

If your pre-set goals do not work as you envisioned them, then learn to be *flexible* in your sales planning. If your goals appear to be far off the mark, consider the following:

- Perhaps they are unrealistic.
- Your staff may not understand them.
- You need to do more extensive market research.
- Your products or service need adjustments.
- Your procedures are too rigid.
- The rewards are too meager.

Any or all of the above could apply.

As anyone who has ever worked with other people knows, *positive reinforcement* is effective. Build your sales staff's confidence instead of dwelling on their weaknesses. The stronger your staff becomes, the more your team will achieve its goals.

Be creative in offering *rewards* to those who reach or surpass their sales goals. A "Sales Executive of the Month" could earn a photo on the bulletin board and a notice in the company's newsletter or in a company press release.

It is always wise to put some *stretch* in your goals and to aim a bit higher than you actually think is realistic. Occasional failure is inevitable, but at least you've aimed high. To aim too low is to encourage poor performance.

Finally, recognize that your staff will have *personal* goals as well as professional ones. When you train or coach about goal setting and planning, don't forget the personal side. Achieving goals in one area of life inevitably leads to strengthening other areas as well. Consider the confidence you felt when you quit smoking, lost weight, or successfully improved a relationship. Didn't your confidence in other areas soar? As one man who set—and reached—a goal of running a marathon said, "Once I did that, I knew I could do just about anything I set out to do." It was a difficult goal, but that made it all the more satisfying when he reached it.

Goals give you a vision of being in a successful situation. Leonard Lauder, president and CEO of Estee Lauder, put it well: "Fantasizing, projecting yourself into a successful situation, is the most powerful means there is of achieving personal goals. That's what an athlete does when he comes onto the field to kick a field goal with 3 seconds on the clock,

80,000 people in the stands, and 30 million watching on TV. The athlete, like the businessman, automatically makes thousands of tiny adjustments necessary to achieve the mental picture he's forming of the successful situation: a winning field goal."

A Matter of Disappointment

About the only downside to goal setting is the sense of disappointment when the goal isn't quite reached. Overall, however, these disappointments are overcome, and new goals are set. No one gets through life without having a goal interrupted. Companies fold unexpectedly, products fail, illness strikes, and natural disasters prevent a company from expanding sales. Ultimately, we can do nothing but pick ourselves up and move on. Fear of disappointment is not a good enough reason for not setting goals.

It's All About Pieces

When you use the SMART formula, you naturally learn to break goals up into manageable pieces. Consider the process of writing a book. The very thought of producing 300 pages of copy can seem overwhelming. But books are written one chapter, indeed one paragraph, at a time, and each chapter can have its own SMART formula applied to it. Given a realistic time frame, the process of writing a book can proceed at its own steady pace. Any professional writer will tell you this is true. And the second book is not nearly as overwhelming as the first. Experience, the great teacher, has paved the way for the next big project.

Training in goal setting is far more effective when the trainee can learn to see all the logical pieces and steps involved in achieving one large goal. Goal setting, like selling or playing golf or any sport, is a skill, and it improves with practice.

In the book *Everyone's a Coach*, by Don Shula and Ken Blanchard, there is a section on the importance of goal setting. Don Shula suspects that most organizations overemphasize this process and don't pay enough attention to what needs to be done to accomplish goals. He feels that follow-up is more important than the goals—the attention to detail, demand for practice perfection, and all the things that separate teams that win from teams that don't.

If you want to be the best sales manager, remember that goal setting only starts good selling behavior. It's your follow-up with your salespeople—your attention to detail and the coaching in the field—that makes it happen.

Effective goal setting rarely happens in a vacuum. It usually thrives in an environment enriched by vision and motivation. That is why goal setting is but one of the "seven secrets" to a successful career in sales management.

> Success is the progressive realization of a worthy goal.
>
> —Earl Nightingale

> If you don't know where you are going, you might wind up someplace else.
>
> —Yogi Berra

> Aiming for perfection is always a goal in progress.
>
> —Thomas J. Watson, IBM

> There are two tragedies in a man's life. One is not having reached one's goal, and the other is having reached it.
>
> —Fred Nietzche

> The destination is marvelous, but the real joy is the journey.
>
> —Bob Small, CEO, Fairmont Hotels

> Since the mind is a specific biocomputer it needs specific instructions and directions. The reason most people never reach their goals is that they don't define them, learn about them, or ever seriously consider them as believable or achievable. Winners can tell you where they are going, what they plan to do along the way, and who will be sharing the adventure with them.
>
> —Dennis Waitely

How to Coach Your Salespeople to Score a Field Goal on Every Sales Call

Goal-getters are go-getters. In a survey conducted not long ago at a prestigious New England graduate school, it was found that 97 percent of the alumni together had made as much money since graduation as the top 3 percent had made as a group.

When the researchers dug deeper, they found that the top 3 percent had clearly definable goals. The goals were specific, measurable, achievable/attainable, realistic, and time-bound (SMART). They had them in college, and they pursued them religiously. The top 3 percent had the unique ability to focus on pre-set goals and to persevere relentlessly in pursuit of those goals.

There are pros and cons to goal-getters. From the company viewpoint, the pros are that these men and women will make the most money for themselves as well as for the firm. They are achievers; you can rely on them to fulfill and exceed their sales quotas.

There are not too many cons to goal setting. The only one to note is the possibility of disappointment.

In goal setting, you need to consider that your salespeople are not *you*. What works for you might not work for them; what motivates you is probably not the same as what motivates them. If you believe strongly in goal setting and want to inculcate that motivation in your salespeople, then you need to learn what goal setting is all about and how to use it.

Here is just some of the accumulated wisdom from a number of motivators, successful entrepreneurs, and my own field experience:

S Specific—Draw your sales and marketing goals clearly and sharply. Focus on specific products and services. Example: Sell 100 dozen units to a specific customer.

M Measurable—All goals must be quantifiable. Example: Get an order from a specific buyer for 40 dozen units.

A Attainable—When starting out, set modest goals that salespeople can achieve, and then build up to higher levels.

R Realistic—The boss needs to be convinced that his or her goals are appropriate and, most of all, realistic. That is, they must be in line with the business economy for the territory.

T Time-bound—All goals must have a time frame for completion in order to determine if the results have been achieved.

Congruent—If your goal setting for the sales team does not coincide with each individual's goal setting, don't be discouraged. Perhaps the team's goals need adjusting. Get the sales team together for some brainstorming. Together you might come up with the answer.

Confidence—Salespeople's confidence increases as they reach each achievable plateau. Goals that are too ambitious set salespeople up for failure, which can mean losing valuable people.

Customized—Goals vary from salesperson to salesperson. What one can achieve, another might find impossible or easy to reach. That's what makes A, B, and C salespeople. Successful goals that those in top management have reached can become sample goals for less successful salespeople if they are explained properly and put into logical perspective.

Experience—Use psychology in "selling" your team goals. There are bound to be those who won't reach them. Not everybody can be first on a sales team. If you want to spur the laggers on to greater goals next month, assure them that failure is not the end of the world and that they can learn from it. Fear of failure can freeze salespeople into total inaction.

Follow-through—Follow-through is essential for success. Following through on your sales plans and letting your sales team know that you are keeping stats on their progress is a smart solution.

Flexibility—Be flexible in your sales planning. If your pre-set goals do not work as you envisioned them, be prepared to make adjustments. If they are too far off the mark, perhaps your goals are too unrealistic or are not understood clearly, you need to do more market research, your products or services need adjustment, your procedures are too rigid, or the rewards are too meager.

Personal goals—Salespeople need to set personal goals as well as business goals. When they successfully reach personal goals, they will be better able to transfer goal setting to business.

Positive reinforcement—Always build on your salespeople's strengths; do not dwell on their weaknesses. The stronger they get, the more of your team's sales goals (and your salespeople's goals) will be achieved.

Rewards—Use creativity to award those whose sales goals have been reached or surpassed. The "Sales Executive of the Month" could earn a photo on the bulletin board, in the newsletter, or in a news release.

Stretch—It is always better to put some stretch in your goals and to aim a little higher. There will be an occasional failure, but it is better than aiming too low and performing poorly.

Goal setting is a lot of work, but the rewards are great for everyone. Successful goals have many ramifications. One of them is, of course, that you can achieve more and make more money. They can also lead to happier salespeople and lower turnover. There is another worthy point: As goals are achieved and everyone benefits, your sales team's regard and respect for you, the coach, and team leader, will grow dramatically.

Goal setting has it's own rewards. Goal getting is only the culmination.

CHAPTER 5

Secret #4: Recruiting, Selecting and Hiring

Andrew Carnegie attributed his success to others whom he had the good sense to hire. He composed the following epitaph for himself: "Here lies one who knew how to get around him, men who were cleverer than himself."

Robert Townsend, in his "Guerrilla Guide" at the back of his best-seller *Up the Organization,* advises executives to hire the best people available. He says that whenever he hired anyone, he would asked himself: "How would I like to work for him—or her—some day?" He also quotes Leo Rosten: "First-rate people hire first-rate people; second-rate people hire third-rate people."

If you ask managers of sales forces to name their two biggest problems, they will tell you:

1. Hiring the "right" people
2. Motivating salespeople to perform at their best

Let's start with hiring the "right" kind of people.

Picking a Winner

Champion racehorses are rarely made; they are bred by champions. Human beings seem to rely on training and conditioning as much as on genetic background. In fact, using the latter as a criterion might be illegal. Picking a winner not only is hard work, but it takes uncommon insight into human nature. Not every salesperson you pick can possibly be a winner. In every event, there can be only one winner, and all the others are runners-up. But with that one winner, or perhaps several high achievers, you make your day—and your year—for a long time.

Unfortunately, there is no foolproof system for picking winners. No human resource department has the magic answer any more than you do. Experience can only raise the percentage of your success. What, then, are some of the criteria for which to look?

First, each applicant comes to you with some kind of a track record. That should tell you something, and it can be checked out quite readily. You must do follow-up and checking or have others, such as the human resource department do it for you.

The next criterion is sort of a gut feeling. If you like the prospect, then chances are your customers will like him or her too. Remember, those first impressions last. But just to make sure, send the applicant you like best up the line to someone else for a second opinion.

Preparation is vital to successful interviewing. Always have the applicant complete an application for your review at least an hour prior to each interview. Then, prepare a group of open-ended questions based on the information listed in each application and the specifications you have developed for the sales territory. Since past performance is an excellent predictor of future performance, questions should be prepared that probe into the applicant's job history.

Next is the actual interview. It should be conversational. Your impressions are no doubt just as valid as a battery of psychological assessment instruments. However, it should be standard operating procedure in your company to have interviewees undergo two such instruments— Interviewing Insights and the Professional Development Sales Profile. These will be discussed in more detail later in this chapter.

Quantity of sales applicants sometimes enables you to arrive at an answer, if selectivity cannot. Conduct at least ten interviews for each opening. This experience will improve your interviewing style as well as help you make more objective comparisons between personalities, impressions, and experiences.

Of course, this is a time-consuming and costly process, but it is far more efficient and effective, and even more economical, than rushing rashly into a decision that could leave you with egg on your face.

One candidate I interviewed came highly recommended from another sales manager within our company. He had extensive product experience and was anxious to step into the sales territory I had open. A battery of psychological assessment instruments were administered by our company psychologist. Everything looked okay, so I hired the person, but in three months I had to terminate him. I was in a hurry, anxious to fill an empty territory, and thought one applicant was enough.

The last step for an applicant who passes your first impression test is to spend a day in the field with two of your best and most-experienced salespeople. Ask both of your salespeople, separately, to give you an evaluation.

Now you are ready for a commitment. Again, remember you cannot pick a winner every time in the hiring process any more than you can at the racetrack. However, the results of personal evaluation and all your personal efforts can surely raise your percentage of winners—and your excellent standing.

Putting the Excel into Excellence

To excel is to reach beyond a quota, above expectations. To excel is to be innovative, diligent, incisive, detail-minded, an aficionado of follow-through. It is great to be successful in selling, but it is greater to excel.

To have a salesperson who excels in his or her job or territory, you have to start out with superior raw material. Many salespeople are on their own once they go out to sell. You might be many miles away, and the training may be finished for the time being. This is when the salesperson's real skills come to the fore.

Some successful marketers place great emphasis on the basic character of a salesperson. Initial interviews, tests, and pre-commitment investigations can determine an individual's integrity, honesty, ambition, and energy. Background checks, including an analysis of the applicant's parents and home life, often reveal astounding information.

When recruiting, it is important establish not only your company goals, but the value systems that you have found to be inherent in those sales reps who have proven to be outstanding.

Having the best staff requires constant searching. Networking in your trade, with outside organizations and associations, and even within your own company often reveals candidates you will want to meet. Perhaps you don't need them today, but tomorrow is always around the corner.

To maintain a staff that excels, it is sometimes necessary to prune. Letting someone go can be more traumatic than hiring people. Unacceptable results and behavior, however, cannot be condoned if you want to build a team that excels—one that works well together, promotes the goals of your company, and makes you look good.

If you accept the premise that building *excel*lence starts with hiring the right people—as well as training them, of course—then you need a working plan that you can follow. Without a business plan, no enterprise can succeed; just as no house can be built without a blueprint.

Recruiting Checklist

A checklist for finding and training skillful salespeople might include the following steps. Mark each subitem that applies to your business.

1. **Identify your industry—**
    (1)   Are there relatively few competitors and a stable product/service situation?
    (2)   Is there new competition and rapidly changing products/services in your future market?

2. **Your product category—Is it:**
    (1)   Capital equipment?
    (2)   Consumer goods?
    (3)   A service?

3. **Technical—**If yours is a technical product, how do you judge your company's support?
    (1)   Strong
    (2)   Average
    (3)   Weak

4. **Product marketing—**How do you believe your company's marketing support shapes up?
    (1)   Strong
    (2)   Weak
    (3)   Relies primarily on salespeople

5. **Future growth interest**—What is your plan to grow?
   (1) Develop more business with present accounts
   (2) Maintain the existing line with established accounts
   (3) Promote new products to new accounts

6. **Time investment**—What budget do you have to hire and train additional sales staff before seeing a return on your investment?
   (1) Six months
   (2) Three to six months
   (3) One to three months

7. **Home office environment**—What type of supervision is available in your home office environment?
   (1) Has a permanent supervisor
   (2) Occasional supervision
   (3) No supervision at all

8. **Prospecting**—Will your salespeople:
   (1) Do their own prospecting?
   (2) Get some help from company efforts?
   (3) Rely completely on other people to do the "bird-dogging" and qualifying?

9. **Training**—How much time will you devote to on-the-job and classroom training of new salespeople?
   (1) Two full weeks or more
   (2) One to two full weeks
   (3) Very little to less than one week

10. **Coaching and counseling**—How much time will you spend in the field with each new salesperson after completing this more intensive training?
    (1) Three days or more
    (2) One to two days
    (3) None to less than one day

After you complete this ten-step questionnaire, add all the "points" you have marked (maximum of 29). Then check the following table to determine the characteristics of the salesperson you need and where you are most likely to find him or her. Your company's human resources department might be grateful for such information.

Salespeople Hiring Chart

Characteristics	If your score is 14 or less	If your score is 15 or less	If your score is 20 to 29
Primary	Tenacity Rapport Work standards Communicator Learner	Leadership Planning Organizing Motivated Interpersonal skills	Persuasiveness Negotiator Analytical Selling skills Organizing Assertive
Secondary	Planning Organizing Motivated Initiative Writer	Analytical Tenacious Communicator Writer Rapport	Responsible and mature Listener Communicator Interpersonal skills Planning
Where best to find such an individual	Look for him or her within the company Recent college graduate	Look for him or her within the company Competitive employment sources	Competitive employment sources

Five Selection Standards and Some Interview Questions for Best Results

While the hiring process might not be conducted on a formal basis or may be handled by others in your organization, the following selection standards and checklist of questions may come in handy if you are called upon to interview a prospective sales applicant (questions may be asked in any order).

Communication and selling skills
1. Tell me about the kind of selling you have been doing.
2. How did you get prospects, and how did you qualify them?
3. How would you sell me if I were one of those prospects? Sell me this ashtray.

Assertiveness and enthusiasm
1. Why did you decide to leave your job with _____?
2. What did you like best about your last position?
3. Why do you think you'd like to work for our company?
4. What do you think would make you more successful in sales?
5. What have you done in the past year to improve yourself?

Interpersonal skills
1. How did you handle customer complaints?
2. What do you consider to be your greatest strengths and weaknesses?

Responsibility and maturity
1. How have you resolved difficult situations with others at _____?
2. How do you feel about working toward a quota?
3. Describe your greatest failure or biggest mistake.

Organizational ability
1. Give me an idea how you spent a typical selling day when you were with _____.

CHAPTER 6

Secret #5: Training the Winners

Learning is the most cost-effective way
to keep your job and prosper in it.

Knowledge is a real bargain. Only ignorance is expensive.

In *creativity,* the sky's not the limit, only imagination.

Stupid is forever, *ignorance* can be fixed.

If you think training is expensive, try *ignorance.*

A winner is someone who recognizes [his or her] other God-given talents, works [his or her] tail off to develop them into skills, and uses these skills to accomplish [his or her] goals.

—Larry Bird

The Seven Principles of Adult Learning

1. People have to recognize their need to learn new information or behavior.
2. New learning should be put to use as soon as possible. Procrastination is the enemy of newly acquired knowledge.
3. People need feedback. Consequences shape behavior.
4. Feedback on an action should come as soon as possible after the action.

5. The environment must allow for trial and error, risk taking, and the possibility of mistakes.

6. Development goals should be divided into steps that are realistic and achievable to avoid discouragement.

7. People should participate in developing their learning goals and in planning how to achieve them.

The ABCs of Verbal and Physical Communication

Communication is the pinnacle of human relations; the lack of communication can be the cause of unending conflicts and misunderstanding. As our society grows and becomes more complex, people are often increasingly separated by a lack of communication. We not only speak different languages but have different perceptions of what we hear.

The following is a list of 26 steps to improved communication. Perhaps none is as important as the "T" factor, which emphasizes empathy. In sales management, few gems of advice are more important than knowing "how to walk in the other person's shoes."

For sales managers, trainers, and salespeople alike, the following A-to-Z list is worth reading and rereading:

A   Avoid confusing words that do not make your meaning clear.

B   Be brief; telegraph your thoughts as if you pay for each word.

C   Clarify meanings by giving more details.

D   Define those terms that might be misunderstood.

E   Emphasize important words to make them jump into the reader's or listener's consciousness.

F   Focus attention on specific activities and requests.

G   Gesture with hands and eyebrows and use other body language for emphasis.

H   Highlight what you think are the key points.

I   Improve steadily; standing still is regressing.

J   Jumping around reduces learning ability; move smoothly from topic to topic.

K   Keep all lines of communication open at all times.

L   Listen while you look at people when you talk to them.

M   Model yourself to your staff in all aspects of behavior.

N   Noise is a detractor to the learning process; eliminate it.

O   Open doors invite openness by those in your charge.

P   Pronounce words clearly and deliberately; it's a good habit.

Q   Question more often than telling; you'll get more answers.

R   Repeat and reemphasize important phrases.

S   Simplify instructions through simple language.

T   Tune in to your listeners; it is called empathy.

U   Use a well-modulated, pleasing voice; listen to yourself, too.

V   Voice your own opinions sparingly and judiciously.

W   Wind up a sales talk with a well-defined request for action.

X   Xtra effort—that little bit—will often win the ball game.

Y   "You" is a wonderful word; use it often with your interviewee.

Z   Zeal is the spark of ambition—and earnings.

Learning to Train

Training others is one of the basic skills of sales managers. This skill brings all of one's experience to the fore. Training is part of the learning process—a four-step procedure that involves:

1. Informing
2. Training
3. Practicing
4. Forming habits

This four-step learning process is entirely natural. The second step and the fifth "secret," *training,* is the focus of this chapter. The following series of principles, or "commandments," will be used as the skeleton to the big body of information and techniques available to achieve optimum results through better training.

1. Training is an empty word without practice. Only doing what they have learned and getting them to change their behavior, will give trainees lasting, usable skills.

2. Managing people means building them up, developing their skills, and giving them knowledge as well as confidence.

3. Give people the credit they deserve. Upstaging them only makes it easier for you to fall off the stage.

4. Let your trainees discover what is new and exciting, and they will be hungry for more and eager to apply their "discovery" to productive efforts.

5. Improve your skills as a recruiter through appropriate techniques, empathy, questions, and understanding of human nature. Being thorough in following up interview claims through reference checking will help.

6. Development as individuals requires plans, tools, and incentives. It is your job to provide them.

7. You are not only a trainer but a catalyst. You can make results happen. You can be the conduit to the success of others—and if they are successful, you will be, too.

8. Train other managers to be trainers. Since "no man is an island," your skills need to be passed on or they will be lost.

9. Be positive at all times, even if faced with a "Pygmalion." Everyone deserves a chance. Sometimes a gem is encrusted with dirt.

10. Always look for what is right, not who is right.

These "commandments" make it easier to focus on the key issues of successful sales training.

Learning to Develop People

The job of training is developing people to improve their performance. In our case, it is a sales manager's job to develop effective salespeople by improving their sales performance. Even those who have years of experience can learn, or relearn, how your company views the job of sales performance training.

Now let's put a little flesh on "The Ten Training Commandments." My comments stem from many years in the profession and from the collective wisdom of others with a similar background.

When will learning ever stop? That's an easy answer:
NEVER! Learning is a lifetime occupation.

The U.S. Post Office affirmed the above adage a dozen or more years ago when it issued a beautiful orange and yellow 15-cent stamp that portrayed a picture, *Glow,* by Josef Albers. The words at the bottom were: "Learning never ends." The blocks of six of these powerful stamps are in the collections of many of my colleagues from the Professional Society for Sales and Marketing Training.

Every manager has a dual responsibility: managing a business and managing people. Managing the business end is a day-to-day job; managing people is a development job. To make sure the business will remain viable some years down the road, you need to nurture people to grow along with you and the business. Like a juggler, you have to keep your eyes constantly on the ball and watch out for little things.

Developing people has to be a selfless job. It means that you are the director, usually behind the scenes, who lets your successful salespeople take the bows. You will hear the applause, too, but most of it will be directed to the people who are front-and-center on the stage. To paraphrase the Bible: "Give credit to your people and you shall accomplish wonders." (The bread cast upon the waters will come back to feed you.)

As a sales manager, you are more of a conduit—a facilitator—than a teacher. Your skills and your experience can help your salespeople learn through training and can motivate them to motivate themselves. Realizing this makes you no less valuable, just a little bit more humble.

To train salespeople, you need to start with trainable people. Pray that the interviewers in the personnel department, or whoever makes hiring decisions (if you do not), pick the right candidates. Previous experience is not always the only basis for selection. Attitude is very important. The man or woman who displays a hunger to learn is a sponge ready and willing to soak up your message.

Frank Bettger, who wrote the very successful book *How I Raised Myself from Failure to Success in Sales,* was once asked why he continued to study so hard. He answered, "Because there is so much I need to learn." He was 78 years old at the time.

Background of Sales Skill Development Curve

When we create a sales performance improvement training program, it is important to focus on enhancing defined sales skills for the sales rep. If such a program were to be designed, we could determine the desired level of proficiency we require from that individual when he or she has completed the program.

Line number 1 of the designed program would represent the various levels of proficiency or sales skills.

Line number 2 would be a horizontal line illustrating the level of proficiency we would demand of the individual upon completion of the sales performance training. Through our initial work with field sales management, we determine that this is an acceptable proficiency level to get the sales job done.

Line number 3 would be a box that signifies the critical period following training where an individual needs to use the new skills daily to incorporate it into current behavior. This is a critical period: the individual is at the skilled apprentice level but requires on-the-job training to move toward the mastery level.

Line number 4 would be the level of a mature sales expert, the desired result. This level implies that salespeople have incorporated sales skills into their formal sales working behavior. They no longer have to think about executing the skill; they just do it. Daily reinforcing and coaching will move a salesperson from the level of simply learning new sales skills to the level of mastering those skills.

This study illustrates the importance of providing coaching after a formal sales performance improvement training program. It is important to provide training just before a salesperson needs to use the skill and to ensure that the next level of sales management is training to reinforce and coach the salesperson on the new set of sales skills. In this way, you have ensured that the salespeople are moving to a mastery level, and you've protected your training dollar. In fact, coaching after sales performance improvement training is the only thing that makes good business sense.

A Four-Step Training Process

Training that has any effect is not mere instruction; rather, it follows a well-defined, tried-and-true process. Use the following four steps to be certain that your trainee actually learns:

1. **Preparation**—Prepare the rep by telling what it is that you are going to teach. Explain why that skill is important and when, where, and how will it be used. Explain what's in it for the rep.
2. **Presentation**—Demonstrate the skill to the rep. Remember, the example teaches.
3. **Application**—Have the rep perform the skill. Correct at once. Compliment good performance. Have the rep explain the steps while performing the skill.
4. **Follow-up**—Review skill usage with the rep frequently. Training without reinforcement is not effective.

As an example, here is a demonstration model on training in the skill of handling objections:

Demonstration Training Model

Skill: Handling objections
Skill Model: Objection handling model
- Listen and observe how the objection is being stated
- Ask for clarification of any misunderstandings
- Rephrase the objection back to the customer or prospect
- Answer the objection with benefits or value pertinent to the objection
- Ask for commitment

1. I'm going to work with you on your skill of handling objections. It's important that you be well-versed in this skill because it can easily lead to the close by simply handling these objections. Many salespeople gloss over this step in the process. As a result, when it is time to close, that objection is still there, and it keeps them from closing the sale.

   Objections can occur at any time during the sales presentation. You must try to handle them when they occur, except if they occur at the beginning of your presentation. Then you must ask your customer to wait and say you will handle the concern later in the presentation.

   Here is what to do when handling an objection:
   - Listen and observe how the objection is being stated
   - Ask for clarification of any misunderstandings

- Rephrase the objection back to the customer or prospect
- Answer the objection with benefits or value pertinent to the objection
- Ask for commitment

2. Demonstrate
   Repeat steps above in No. 1.

3. Have someone in the class demonstrate the model using a role-playing situation.

4. Inform the trainees that you will be checking back to observe how they are handling objections.

Developing a salesperson also follows a well-defined path with five logical steps: Trainees need:

1. **Expectations**—To know what is expected of them

2. **Opportunities**—Chances to perform in order to gain hands-on learning and retention

3. **Feedback**—So they will know how they are doing; otherwise, improvement will be slow, if not impossible

4. **Assistance**—If and when required, and confidence that you will be there

5. **Rewards**—For good results

The actual trainers in any sales organization are the field sales managers or district sales managers, as they are designated in many companies. They are closest to the salespeople and immediately available if assistance is needed. If the organization is large enough to have field or district sales managers, then it is important to *train these trainers.* They will be your conduits to increased performance, which results in increased sales.

An assigned territory becomes the sales representative's domain. To maximize the territory's potential, the sales manager and representative must be in constant communication. Many things can and do happen outside of the territory that affect business emanating from it:

- Changing demographics
- The possibility of a branch opening
- A political or zoning development that could impact sales activities

On the other hand, the sales representative can spot actual or impending changes from ground-level observances, such as:

- Personnel changes in the customer or prospect's offices
- Competitive pressures and changes
- Media and display opportunities
- New local industries
- Changes in local product or service preferences

Information from both sides must be exchanged at all times and become part of the sales manager's planning. The recording of all such information by the sales manager is important for yet another reason. What if the sales representative decides to leave? Without a detailed database, the sales manager and the company would have to start all over again amassing vital strategic information.

There is also an ethical issue to address: Do not concern yourself with *who* is right in a situation fraught with potential conflict, but *do* what is right. Your company's reputation is at stake. You need to exercise uncommon wisdom to arrive at the correct answers. Rely on your sales rep, but rely on yourself and your good sense more. The following acronym was gleaned from well-known author, speaker, and consultant Richard F. Gerson:

H E L M—Be Honest, Ethical, Legal, and Moral.

Learning from Experience

It has been said that experience is a great teacher. Sales trainer Jack Falvey wrote a pertinent article, "Speaking from Experience," for the American Society for Training and Development's journal. In it, he capsulizes, in three steps, the salesperson's needs to learn:

1. Sales representatives must be students of their customers' business—remembering that "people buy from people" and not from companies. This means continuous study because customer needs are always changing.
2. Sales representatives must be students of applications of their product in the customer's business. Remember that it is not the product's specifications that clinch the sale, but its performance. The "why" and "what" of the results must be the focus.

3. Sales representatives must be students and expert practitioners of selling skills. These skills must be built in actual selling conditions, not just in practice sessions.

Training, then, is not done in a one-time session; it is a continuous process in the field. Sales management must convince the sales staff that this continuous process is carried out primarily by them. Sales managers can only provide the basic structure, some tools, the motivation, and ongoing supervision, but they provide the conduits to continuous learning.

Show your staff two simple tools that will help them learn from experience:

1. A 3 ×5 card listing each customer's buyer information data, objective for the call, and a brief sales record
2. An account management folder that contains updated information on key personnel, buying history, and results that can help future sales efforts

The sales manager should also keep a copy of this information in the company's file, update it, and add it to the salesperson's file as well.

Ed Finn, another outstanding sales trainer, shared the following with members of the Professional Society for Sales and Marketing Training:

> CUSTOMER PROFILE—PERSONAL, developed by John J. McCarthy. In the Appendix is some "Leaner Controlled Instruction," using a bio of Paul Edwards provided by Ed. This bio can be changed to your industry. I created a version of this wherein Paul is President of the True Benefit Hardware Company... completely different industry and career background but with the same personal data.

This approach is effective in helping salespeople recognize and adapt to those unique things that make people behave as they do. In using this training technique, several salespeople, as they begin to read Paul M. Edwards, have said, "Hey, I know this guy." Their observation and reaction skills are sharpened as they "listen with their eyes."

Experience costs money and time, and if we do not learn from it, we would be fools, indeed. Ben Franklin said it first in *Poor Richard's Almanac* (1757):

Experience keeps a dear school,
but fools will learn in no other.

Learning to Delegate

You might think that once you are the sales manager, you will find it easy to tell other people to take over some of the jobs. Surprisingly, you will not find it easy. Delegating is a learned art.

Why do we hesitate to let others do some of the lesser tasks? Our own insecurity? Distrust of others? Too much trouble to train others? We're not sure how to do it ourselves and want to try and find out first?

One or all of the above reasons are true. Yet, why have we become sales managers if not to direct others, which then allows us more time for planning and thinking. The executive functions are ours now. Sales management is our job; selling is theirs.

The salesperson to whom you have delegated the job of selling will increase the sales performance qualities that you have delegated to him or her. The salesperson will ideally develop from a dependent, low-level sales representative to an independent, highly competent performer. Delegation is a gradual process that will enhance the salesperson's self-esteem and individual worth to the organization.

When you delegate a task to another employee, you're both a coach and a matchmaker. You are a coach because you are instructing the salesperson in the specific task, telling him or her exactly how to perform it. You are matching the requirements of the delegated task with the known or assumed capabilities of the salesperson. Your ability to instruct and exercise good judgment as a matchmaker will enable the person to whom you have delegated to succeed most of the time. Don't expect 100 percent success, but be there if your support is needed. No growth is possible without risking some failure.

Delegating also assumes that you have confidence in the person, and this encouragement and reassurance will generate confidence. But most of all, it will free you from having to do those tasks yourself. Having more time for your growth is the ultimate result of sound delegation.

Apply the following two exercises in delegation to your situation. Remember that delegation is not instinctive; it is a learning process.

Delegate Clearly

What to Do	How to Do It
1. Determine the results you expect before you make the assignment.	1. Consider the specific "deliverable" in terms of what it will look like, what it will contain, what sales results expected, and when it is required. If there is a vision or image in your mind that reflects the kind of job you want, describe that image. If the task is vague, state at least some components that will be specific, that may provide a bridge to the next step. Test your view of the expected results against similar tasks or projects; ask your manager to help refine your view of what must be accomplished.
2. Make standards clear, so that salespeople know precisely what constitutes a mistake or unsatisfactory performance.	2. Outline specifically and quantitatively the degree of accuracy, timeliness, neatness, completeness, cost, and so on required in an assignment.
3. Identify the limits of authority in delegation.	3. Identify the kinds of decisions the salespeople can make and those that you will make. Make surfe the salespeople understand this difference.
4. Help salespeople anticipate the mistakes that are likely to occur and what to do about them.	4. Review assignments step by step. Identify potential weak points in the process, and develop a list of potential obstaqles to be overcome. Brainstorm ways for surmounting these obstacles.

Delegate According to Your Salespeoples' Skill Level

What to Do	How to Do It
1. Become familiar with your employees' skill level.	1. Keep formal or informal skill inventories on your salespeople and update them regularly. Avoid stereotyping a salesperson's skill level. Do not permanently label someone as a poor closer, for instance, based on one or two incidents.
2. Identify the most common mistakes particular salespeople tend to make and the areas in which they have strength.	2. Using a skill inventory or a job description, rate individuals on areas of strength and weakness. Predict what effect deficiencies will have on performance.
3. Give salespeople advice about handling selling situations where you suspect they might make errors or need support.	3. Make suggestions on potential trouble areas. Ask the salesperson what can be done to avoid mistakes in these areas. Offer your interpretation of what can be done to avoid errors.

Learning to Change Behavior Through Experience

Each sales call, especially a first-time call, is a new situation for your sales reps. They may not know the best way to present themselves. What they usually do is choose a tactic with which they are familiar, apply it, and hope for the best. If it works, then it stays in their bag of tricks; if it doesn't, then it's tossed, and a new approach is tried. This is what trial and error is all about. However, trial and error can be expensive, as common as it is.

Regrettably, this trial-and-error method is more commonplace than we might like to see. It is also expensive. An old adage tells us that experience may not be worth what it costs, but we can't seem to get it for any less. Not true! *Training* helps us get experience for a lot less.

Training is aimed at reducing, if not eliminating, costly errors in time, money, and loss of productivity. Learning through training can become a company-wide, cumulative process from which everyone benefits. It is a win–win situation for the company and your salespeople.

How do you erase the errors of inexperience? In other words, as the sales manager, how can you make training—learning—more effective?

The Four Levels of Learning

First, it is important to understand the four levels of learning:

1. Unconscious incompetence (informing)
2. Conscious incompetence (training)
3. Conscious competence (practicing)
4. Unconscious competence (habit)

Level 1: Unconscious incompetence (informing)—When you first learned to drive a car, you were in the informing stage. You not only didn't know how to drive, but you didn't know why you didn't have this skill. You were unconscious about your incompetence.

Level 2: Conscious incompetence (training)—As you began your training, you suddenly gained some knowledge and became consciously aware of your lack of competence. You knew why you couldn't drive.

Level 3: Conscious competence (practicing)—After several lessons, you learned various steps—putting the key in the ignition, using the gas pedal and the brakes, steering, etc. With some practice, you begin to become aware of your competence as a driver. Through constant practice, you learned to understand the process that makes a car run safely. Each time you drove, you had to be consciously aware of every mental and physical part of the process, but you were driving.

Practice is the most difficult phase of the learning process, and your trainees may want to give up. This is natural, because it is also the most stressful phase. This is when they try to implement new behaviors, and they initially perform them imperfectly. They want to go back to their old, more comfortable ways of doing things, even if those old ways aren't very effective. They need to understand that it is okay for them to make mistakes during this practice phase, because that is how practice leads to improvement. Sales training programs that include role playing and field coaching work best during the practicing level of learning.

Level 4: Unconscious competence (habit)—Think about the last time you drove a car. Were you consciously aware of steering, accelerating, braking, or shifting gears? Probably not. After driving for a while, most of us progress to a level of habitual performance. We can drive skillfully without actively thinking about all the steps we perform. They come naturally. After all that practice, we can drive on automatic pilot, and our practice results in assimilation and habit. We are now considered at the level of Unconscious Competence in driving.

This four-level model can be used to train your sales reps in learning any new sales process.

The Seven Areas of Training New Salespeople

I sought the opinions of a representative group of sales managers (primarily those concerned with marketing of industrial goods) to find out where vestibule (beginning) salespeople could best learn their profession. In order of preference, here are the seven areas the respondents thought were the most important training areas:

1. **Training about the company**—History, organization, policies, personnel:
   a. First choice: office work experience at company headquarters
   b. Second choice: at regular sales meetings
   c. Third choice: workshop sessions
2. **Training about the product**—Materials, design, performance:
   a. Plant work experience
   b. Office work experience
   c. Classroom or workshop experience
3. **Training about the selling process**—The ways to influence customers (communication/presentation skills, probing, objection handling, negotiation, and closing):
   a. Classroom sales training course
   b. On the job, with an experienced person
   c. At regular sales meetings

4. **Training about customer service/satisfaction—**
   a. On the job under an experienced customer-service employee
   b. At regular sales meetings
   c. On the job by oneself

5. **Training about competitive lines—**
   a. On the job, with an experienced person
   b. At regular sales meetings
   c. In classroom or workshop

6. **Training about engineering—**Technical training in a classroom or workshop situation
   a. University-level engineering training
   b. Plant work experience
   c. Classroom or on-the-job training under an experienced person

7. **Training about business principles—**Economics, marketing, accounting, production:
   a. College degree in business administration or liberal arts
   b. Office work experience, particularly in a sales office
   c. Classroom work (academic)

The consensus of this study showed that participation in plant or office activities was far more realistic than observer status. Managers also agreed that it was unwise and too costly to start a salesperson out by himself or herself. All participants in the study considered realistic, hands-on work superior as a learning climate to academic (classroom) work alone.

The AICCF Formula

This formula celebrates its golden anniversary and may be even older. At the beginning of World War II, the War Production Board formulated steps for greater efficiency and effective selling. A dozen years later, the Small Business Administration disseminated this wisdom once again. More than a generation later, AICCF is still a viable and useful formula to teach effective steps in selling:

A   is for *analysis* of the customer's needs and for gaining his or her attention.

I   is for arousing the customer's *interest* through the accurate selection of goods and services to meet his or her needs.

C   is for *convincing* customers, by demonstration or other proof, that your product or service is the best solution to their needs.

C   is also for *closing* the sale or getting the contract.

F   is for *follow-up* to make sure that the results promised actually materialized and the customer is happy—and primed for the next sale.

The AMPSA Formula

For at least two generations, industrial psychologists have applied the AMPSA formula to the learning process. A lot of skilled research went into its development, and it is also certainly worth trying.

A   stands for getting the learner's *attention.*

M   stands for *motivating* the learner.

P   stands for *participation* by the learner.

S   stands for *satisfaction* that the learner should derive from training.

A   stands for *application* of the theory to a real situation.

Let's look at the first step: *attention.* Learners are exposed to a great many ideas each day, all competing for their attention. They might be perturbed about bad news from their hometown. A child might be sick at home. A spouse may have complained about something that morning. And there you are trying to help your salespeople not be defensive when a prospect says, "Your price seems pretty steep to me!"

Are they really listening to your wise words? They might be repeating them as you have asked them to do, but is this information sinking in? Is it becoming part of their inventory of knowledge that they can taken on the road.

One way to make sure they hear and understand is to be specific. Generalization merely washes over their consciousness. Pin your examples to specific, credible, realistic situations that have personal meaning. *That* is getting attention.

On to *motivation* and *participation*, which go together. Motivation can be achieved through participation. Your trainees might repeat your advice, argue about it, discuss it, add to it, or apply it to a situation from their experience. If they do any of these things, they are participating—and motivated.

Learning by doing is a sound educational principle. It is acting from imagination, and the results are retention and future application. Actual doing helps implant your training in the learner's mind. Discussion and even arguments about the new behavior help to accelerate the training. This active participation during the learning process helps create a belief in the learner's mind that it was his or her idea after all. There is no motivation like self-satisfaction. *Satisfaction* then becomes the reward.

The selling behavior you have taught now belongs to the trainees if they have paid *attention,* were properly *motivated,* and *participated* in the learning process. Your trainees should feel good about their new knowledge and the favorable results it will have on their income and self-esteem. The trainees now have become unconsciously competent and have a new habit.

Application is the final phase of this behavioral learning process. This phase is perhaps the most important, because this is the chance to apply what has been learned to the actual selling operation. Training technique is only as good as the extent to which it moves from the theoretical realm to the practical situation. Your trainees must apply what they have learned in order to bridge the gap. Follow-up can determine whether they have indeed had their ears and minds open, and an increased paycheck is pragmatic, demonstrable proof.

The entire training process often revolves around changing behavior that has not been productive in the past. The most effective method is the dramatic case method, which is presenting a problem and then acting out its solution, much like acting out a play. It is also like illustrating a story in a book in that it calls in another sense, the eyes as well as the ears. When more of our senses are involved in the learning process, the ability to retain information is enhanced.

Active participation also provides emotional stimulation and reinforces the learning process. A group setting helps develop a sense of belonging to the company. As a follow-up, take a look at the trainees' commission checks during pay periods. If you see them increase, you know they've got it made—and so have you.

> Don't' be afraid to take a big step You can't cross a chasm in two small jumps!
>
> —David Lloyd George, British statesman

> There is very little difference in people, but that little difference is attitude. The big difference is whether it is positive or negative.
>
> —W. Clement Stone (Mark Twain)

Learning About Communication

Sometimes it seems that business correspondence is dead. If that's true, then executives have killed it. Computers, facsimiles, and e-mail frequently take the place of business letters.

When you write a personal letter to a customer, supplier, official, or fellow executive, do you expect a reply? Of course you do. Unfortunately, most of the time your letter is ignored.

Over the past year, I have taken my own informal survey. I kept copies of letters that were directed personally to vital people in a variety of industries, companies, media, and government bureaus. I had a 25 percent response to my letters. A few follow-up phone calls, however, produced recognition of our letter contact and resultant answers—by voice, not by letter.

Recently, I met an executive of a large company who had the reputation of being "a nice guy" and a highly effective, successful representative of his firm. He had responded to my letter and subsequently invited me to meet him at his office. I asked about his success and expressed my thanks for his quick written reply.

"This is part of my job," he said. "I make it a policy to answer all serious personal letters as quickly as I can." There are few frustrations in business that equal an ignored letter inquiry. Is it the secretary's fault? Is the person you wrote too busy? Too busy with what? Alibis do not a sale make.

Correspondence is a serious and often neglected form of human communication. Perhaps it is old-fashioned, but then so are courtesy, honesty, and ethics. As a sales manager and trainer, it will be important for you to pass on this advice: A five-minute letter and a single postage stamp can germinate into a thousand-dollar profit. At the very least, it can open a door at some time in the future, create a friend in need, build an image for you and your company that will overcome competition, and be the bread cast upon the waters that could someday come back to feed you.

The Cost of Training New Salespeople

In a mobile, fast-changing environment like the United States, an annual turnover of 20 percent is about average. It means that one-fifth of a sales force is new each year, and performance improvement sales training becomes a constant expense.

According to a 1992 survey by the Dartnell Corporation of Chicago, small companies (those generating less $5 million in revenues) spent about four months training each new sales representative, at a cost of $5,530. Larger companies spent even more and often took longer before they put their new reps on the road. The average annual training cost for all companies was $6,226 per person.

Thanks...For the Memory!

Psychologist Douglas Herrmann developed a series of hints on how to improve one's memory. There are few tools as valuable to learning new and better ways of selling—or doing almost anything—as a finely tuned memory. Here are a few valuable suggestions:

- When you meet someone for the first time, repeat the person's name and look him or her in the eyes. Try to repeat the name again during your conversation and when parting. You might say, "Joe Jones, it has been a pleasure meeting you." Following the meeting, write the name in your address book or wherever you maintain such records. The act of writing also reinforces memory.

- Use the power of association. Associate the way a person looks or acts with something you can remember easily. For example, "Joe always has his hair in a crew cut, so now I associate Joe as Joe 'crew cut' Jones."

- Practice recall of several situations at once to sharpen your ability to memorize. Herrmann refers to former President Lyndon B. Johnson, who used to watch three different television sets at once to catch news reports from different networks.

- Space out the task of memorizing. Don't try to memorize everything at once, as students often do on the evening prior to an exam. Study a small portion each day; it'll stay with you longer.

- Limit stress and tension. These states are destructive, distracting, and make you forgetful.

- We all have certain peak hours when we are at our best. Most people seem to be most alert between 11 A.M. and 4 P.M. and at their best on Fridays and Saturday. It would appear that these times are best for working on memory tasks.

- If you need to be especially alert at an event, avoid drinking alcohol, smoking, drinking caffeine beverages, eating too much, not getting enough sleep before the event, and taking long trips across time zones.

- The positive things you can do to optimize your memory are get a good night's sleep, do light exercises, enjoy a balanced diet, and practice physical relaxation. Nutrition researchers have found that recall can be improved, especially when studying, by drinking lemonade sweetened with sugar, which provides a combination of vitamin C and energy.

Learn by Teaching; Teach by Learning

Set an example for salespeople by creating a learning agenda for yourself. Actively gather information from inside and outside the company on one or two issues at a time. Don't be afraid to say, "I don't understand what you mean; please run that by me again."

Leaders who respect others' expertise and show a commitment to learning command respect themselves.

—Calhoun W. Wick,
The Learning Edge: How Smart Managers
and Smart Companies Stay Ahead

To teach is to learn twice.

—Joseph Joubert

Experience is a good teacher, but she sends in terrific bills.

—Minna Autrim

CHAPTER 7

Secret #6: Coaching Your Team

A sales manager is a person who is able to manage sales. This may sound simplistic, but it is not. If these professionals were not able to manage, they would be out knocking on doors. However, because they are able to inspire others to perform at their best, they will lead them on to continued successes.

Sales managers act as a catalyst rather than as supersalespersons. They make it possible for the company to make a profit, for their sales representatives to make a good living, and to satisfy customers.

Sales managers are also the orchestrators of a unique symbiotic arrangement. As such, they blend the requirements of the company with the needs of their salespeople and the demands of the customer. They blend these needs into a smooth, harmonious process.

Sales managers are also able to be jacks-of-all-trades, so to speak. They know the techniques of selling, but they also understand how to train—to motivate others to do well and even better. On top of that, they are the ambassadors who represent the company at trade shows. They are administrators who don't shirk the often onerous task of getting the administrative paperwork done. Finally, they are receivers of all that is new, innovative, and informative. They call the play that can win the ball game; they are coaches who have the vision to mold their salespeople into a winning team.

Technically, coaching is a management development program in which a junior executive works directly under a senior executive. In sales management, coaching is the face-to-face process that helps you analyze and improve the performance of the salespeople you manage. It is the regular input that you, the boss, give to the individuals on the sales force. It is the daily guidance about how to do the job.

Coaching is leading. Leading is teaching. Teaching is motivating. Coaching is what the top managers of athletic teams do to get their charges to perform at optimum levels—and to win ball games. In athletics, the reward is winning, being able to play more instead of hugging the bench or even signing a million-dollar contract.

In a unique way, sales managers hold the key to overcoming the all too common problem of the failure of salespeople. That key is coaching—the coaching sales managers provide to those they manage and, equally important, the way in which they provide that coaching. It means showing salespeople specific ways to change their behavior and thus improve. This will help them reach not only the company's goals but their own goals—to satisfy their needs, be happy, and make a lot of money.

When sales managers coach their salespeople, they must keep three ideas in mind to lead their team to better results:

1. A good manager gets things done through others.

2. You get paid for what your salespeople bring in, not for what you do.

3. If you are honest with yourself, you will find that you need your salespeople more than they need you.

You need to be the coach, to provide the game plan for your team, and to do everything possible so that your salespeople will be successful.

As a manager, you are in charge of results, which are often related to earnings. One of the major costs of sales management is finding and training salespeople. Because the cost of hiring and training is so expensive, it stands to reason that replacement is a luxury you need to avoid if at all possible. Proper coaching, which sometimes includes behavior modification, is much more economical and effective than replacement.

Rules of Good Coaching

Good coaches:

- Know that *no sales force is perfect,* yet they want to pursue that impossible dream.

- Know that *coaching occurs constantly*—formally and informally—but on a planned basis.

- Have clearly defined *standards of performance.* It is helpful but not essential that coaches meet or surpass those standards. They probably did so on the way up to their present position.

- *Operate from the sidelines,* fully understanding that they can't coach and play at the same time.

- Recognize, understand, and accept *individual* differences and know the fallacy of attempting to make all sales team members act the same or act like the coach.

- Appreciate the value of the "university of hard knocks" and use it as a coaching tool.

- Know that people learn best by doing and then by understanding, learning from, and living with the results.

- Are most effective when respected. If employees have respect for the coach's abilities and accomplishments and the results they have produced, they will respond to coaching efforts. If respect is lacking, coaching is ineffective.

- Don't look for miracles. They are willing to be satisfied with steady, average progress, with success that comes a phase at a time but shows gradual and lasting progress.

- Know that the single most important possession of human beings is a favorable image of themselves. Coaching is very important in developing a salesperson's self-image.

The Skills of Good Coaching

To harness the power of good coaching skills, you need to have well-developed skills in six areas:

1. Principles of professional selling
2. Communication
3. Motivation
4. Counseling
5. Good judgment
6. Leadership: using the talents available on your team

Principles of Professional Selling

There is a very close relationship between the principles of professional selling and good sales management coaching. Here are a few examples to demonstrate:

- **Knowledge**—Know your product and know it well. Sales managers have been preaching this to their salespeople for years. In coaching we say, "Know your subject well." Be sure to know all areas of the subject that you are going to be coaching. In addition, know the people you are coaching and know them well. Know their needs, wants, and aspirations as individuals. Without this critical people knowledge, you are working in the dark.

- **Benefits**—Know the benefits of your product or service. Know how the customer will benefit by using your product or service. The application to your coaching efforts is obvious; you will be a more effective coach and will obtain better results if you point out to people the obvious benefits of changing their behavior—and doing what it is you want them to do.

- **Perseverance**—Sales managers have been preaching that perseverance is a key ingredient in selling success. They remind their salespeople that 85 percent of their big ticket sales are made after the fifth "no" and encourage them to persevere and not become discouraged. This also applies to coaching. Good coaches do not look for perfection. They realize that coaching takes time as well as a great deal of patience and perseverance.

- **Long term versus short term**—For many years, sales managers have been telling their salespeople to "work for the long term, not just for today's sale." That advice can easily be applied to coaching. Daily coaching tips and advice should contribute to longer term goals, for both the coach and the trainees.

- **Respect**—Always earn the respect of the customer. That's another maxim sales managers have stressed for years. If you have the respect of the customer, your selling job will be easier. When the coach has the respect of the employee, coaching, too, becomes easier.

- **Sales call planning**—Plan every part of the selling situation. Have an objective for everything you do or say. When you make a sales call, have a SMART call objective for that call. Reaching each day's objective should contribute to reaching the long-range objective that you have for each customer. That's good advice for both the sales manager and the coach. (See the Coaching Visit—Planning Worksheet at the end of this chapter.)

- **Sincerity**—Develop a genuine interest in your customers so that they will trust you, have confidence in you, and know that you are genuinely concerned about them and their well-being. This is also an excellent guideline for successful coaching.

There is an obvious interrelationship between the principles of professional selling and the role of the coach as a developer of people.

Communication

So much electronic gadgetry is available today that regular written communication appears to be going the way of the dinosaur. Yet there is still no substitute for the direct personal letter. It is regrettable that less than 50 percent of business correspondence ever gets answered. Computer messages, fax transmissions, e-mail, and voice mail all get preferential treatment over the ordinary 32-cent business letter.

One of the first things a sales manager should do is equip his or her field staff with personalized correspondence pads and a supply of stamped envelopes and then encourage them to communicate with their customers. For example, they can:

- Tell them when they will be visiting them
- Thank them after a sales call
- Write a kind word to anyone who is helpful in making an introduction or facilitating a sale (i.e., a receptionist or secretary, who can often help close a sale)
- Send birthday wishes, holiday greetings, or congratulations to the decision makers and their assistants

All of these communications can be most helpful in building a unique image and an advantage for your salespeople.

Dropping an occasional note to a customer and making a suggestion, revealing a sales secret, or passing along information about the competition can be one of the marks of an excellent salesperson. Of course, a fax is faster and even preferred within some companies, but it just doesn't have the personal warmth of a letter. It's like the difference between a handshake and a hug.

One of the problems with writing a letter these days is that it requires a skill many people either don't have or they think they don't have. However, writing is like talking. Smooth writing reads much like conversation sounds. It is the same language, but different tools are used.

When it comes to answering inquiries or any kind of correspondence, an important principle applies. The longer you wait to answer an inquiry, the greater the chance that you won't answer it at all. A good rule to follow for personal or business correspondence is answer it today. It will only take half as long as doing it next week, when the topic is cold and it's more difficult to think of what you want to say.

Motivation

This such an important subject that Chapter 8 is devoted to it.

Counseling

As a sales manager (or someone in a higher management position), you have less to do with actually making the sale. Therefore, you have to create a working environment that will help your people to motivate themselves. If they are motivated and do their jobs well, then you will be successful.

Motivating others is a little like being a psychologist. You must get into other people's heads to analyze what makes them tick and to figure out how to give them incentives to improve.

Pre-Call Coaching and Post-Call Coaching

Some sales managers call this "curbstone coaching." These two effective techniques are used in the field before and after sales calls to motivate salespeople to make adjustments and improvements in their selling skills.

In *pre-call coaching,* have the salesperson visualize each sales call before actually making it. Ask:

- Why are you making this call?
- Do you have a call objective?

- Is it specific, measurable, attainable, realistic, and time-bound?
- Whom are you going to see? (Decision maker or others who have influence in the buying decision?)
- What are you going to present?
- How are you going to do this?
- Why should the customer buy what you are presenting?
- What visual aids, success stories, and/or testimonials do you plan to use?
- If you expect the customer to raise any objections, how will you overcome them?

A pre-call practice session should also consider the salesperson's appearance, body language, and behavior. Information and tact are called for to make this a motivating session.

Post-call coaching is the feedback each salesperson needs, particularly if the sales manager, trainer, or mentor has observed the salesperson in action. This coaching will be more effective if it takes place soon after the sales call, when the experience is still fresh.

A sales manager might use the following questions during a post-call coaching session:

1. Did you achieve your call objective? If so, what did you do to achieve it? If not, what could you have done differently?
2. What objections were raised? How well did you handle them?
3. How often did you close? What reaction did you get?

Consultative-type selling is advising, not doing. This is a difficult concept for sales managers to grasp who have come up the ladder from the field. The manager's job is to advise the sales staff, to help them represent the company and its products and services in the most favorable light, and to maximize both company profits and the salesperson's income.

Consultative selling for the 1990s is a bit different from what it was in prior decades. (The requirements of this decade will be discussed more fully later.) The greatest myth about salespeople is that they are supposed to possess the "gift of gab," but modern consultative selling introduces a twist: less talk, more listening. This might be more difficult, but recent studies of effective selling techniques confirm that the more successful salespeople talk less and listen more.

Listening to the customer allows salespeople to determine the customer's real needs and find the "hook" that will make the sale. Being persuasive, goal-oriented, pertinent, and empathetic is key. Coaching sales trainees accordingly will make them more effective in the long run.

Some other important concepts of modern consultative selling include *benefits, results, value-added,* and *closing.* These old standbys have been around for quite some time.

Benefits, or the "selling of benefits," has been the darling of pop psychologists. Many sales managers and trainers now say that this is an overworked cliché. They prefer to use the terms *value-added* or *results.*

1. A benefit, says one national trainer, is only a benefit if the person hearing it perceives it to be a benefit at the very instant it is mentioned. *Results* are different. The use of that term forces the salesperson to think about what he or she can deliver in terms the customer can better digest. *Value-added* is similar, except that it brings in the value that the salesperson or the company is adding to what was already inherent in the product or service.

2. Talking about results:
   a. Helps customers envision something positive and desirable that can happen if they take your offer
   b. Helps them perceive the end result of buying from you
   c. Encourages them to take action on your proposal

The other modern "no-no" phrase is "closing a sale." It is now being supplanted by a more up-to-date phrase, "getting a commitment." The word *close* implies a conclusion, an end to your doing business with the customer, rather than *opening up* a fresh or ongoing relationship. *Closing a sale* implies finality.

Closing has been psychologically associated with the pushy old-timer who put his foot in the door so it would not be closed on him. Companies looking for "strong closers" are probably high-pressure outfits you may not want to be associated with. Getting a definite, specific, strong commitment assumes a different attitude. It can mean that the sale is approved, and it can also mean that:

• Your proposal will be placed before the buying or marketing committee

• You will get a crack at an order when current inventories run low

- Your sample will get fair testing and consideration
- Your name will be on the next "Invitation to Bid" or "Request for Proposal" list

Encourage your salespeople to talk about results; it will help them get a commitment. This technique is likely to become the way of doing business for the 1990s and beyond.

Good Judgment

How do you acquire good judgment? Where can you study up on it? Exercising good judgment is part psychology, part experience, and a whole lot of common sense.

Judgment, according to the *American Heritage Dictionary,* is "the mental ability to perceive and distinguish relationships...the capacity to form an opinion by distinguishing and valuating...the formation of an opinion after consideration or deliberation." A synonym is *reason.* The *PUNdit's Dictionary* says it is "the ability to put brain in gear before putting tongue in motion."

Astute salespeople know almost instinctively, and certainly by experience, that the customer is the focus of their mature judgment. Correctly analyzing the buyers of their products and services is one of the highest goals of their profession. The fruits of judgment or analysis will show up on their sales reports; next to the order, this is perhaps their most valuable contribution to the sales manager's records.

Judging the customer is a prime tool in the professional salesperson's arsenal of skills. Sales managers must therefore keep the customers in focus when designing sales training programs in order to enhance this ability to judge. Some of the topics a sales training program should include are:

- Identifying specific customer needs
- Training sales reps in current customer needs, especially in technical capabilities
- Training customers' service personnel
- Training suppliers
- Implementing Total Quality Management

- Having an open-door and open-mind policy toward learning as well as changes occurring in the marketplace
- Creating a versatile, cross-functional sales force with a team mentality
- Keeping everyone informed and updated on corporate responsibilities that reflect company policy—with emphasis on ethics, environment, quality, responsibility, and reliability

It is a difficult assignment for sales management to accept the judgment of the salesperson, but it is as necessary as complete training and indoctrination. British statesman Edmund Burke recognized this two centuries ago when he said:

> Your representative owes you not his industry only, but his judgment; and he betrays, instead of serves you, if he sacrifices it to your opinion.

Leadership

Leadership is the sixth coaching skill, and it, too, is hard to define. Some call it charisma, used both for good and evil; some call it having a vision; and others relate it to respect and integrity. It is all of these often subtle characteristics, yet it is identifiable even in a crowd of peers.

Leadership is the art of bringing out the best in the people you lead. It starts with training and with motivating your representatives to perform at their best level. It includes supplying them with the necessary technical know-how, with enthusiasm for the job and with an understanding of customer psychology. It includes treating people with integrity and honesty and putting them first, just as you expect your sales staff to put the customer first.

Occasionally, leadership will include accompanying a salesperson to see a client, but the sales manager should take a back seat by listening rather than leading the interview. The manager's presence will add confidence to the sales rep's efforts and impress the customer with the importance of the mission. As soon as possible after the call, the manager should debrief the salesperson, asking probing questions in a non-critical way.

Like good coaches, leaders, in this case sales managers, will help staff reach corporate goals, but should not carry the ball themselves.

A Sales Manager is a cheerleader, not a quarterback. For a company to grow, a Sales Manager can't spend time managing sales; he or she should manage the people who make the sales.

—Jack Falvey, Intermark

Coaching Problems and Solutions

Coaches must lead their sales teams to the highest level of performance. Sometimes the players, being human, fall short of projected goals, or external circumstances totally beyond the control of the coaches and the team get in the way. Occasionally, internal conflicts interfere, which, while not the fault of the sales team, nevertheless have an impact on its success. For each of these "problems," coaches must find a solution. Their solutions may not always be successful, but it is their job to try.

Let's look at some typical situations and how they might be resolved:

The Problem	A Possible Solution
Sales are declining despite the usual efforts. This has been going on for at least a month.	You need to take the initiative and be proactive. If you have ruled out uncontrollable outside influences (a slump in the economy, war, epidemic, changes in technology, fashion trends, consumer approval), call your staff together and get a consensus on fresh starts. Their jobs are on the line, as is yours.
You have made a mistake. News of your bad decision has gotten around and lowered your credibility as a manager.	Well, you're human, aren't you? Perhaps you have been "going like sixty" when your engine is only made to "run at fifty." Stop making quick decisions; delegate more chores so that you will have more time to consider your actions. Study possible results. Review your plans and goals to make sure they are still realistic, and make changes if necessary. And don't forget that you, too, are part of a team. Ask your teammates for input. Listen to other points of view. Sometimes it gets lonely at the top.
Some very simple problems: The delivery per-	Simple problems? Like a splinter in the sensitive tip of your finger! The sad thing is that

The Problem	*A Possible Solution*

son dumped the order unceremoniously on the customer's doorstep and was impolite. The bookkeeper gave a snippish answer when attempting to collect a bill. The shipping clerk was careless in packing and the item arrived damaged. The salesman, despite three calls from the unhappy customer, did not call back.

such little molehills become insurmountable mountains. All of a sudden, the offended customer stops placing orders—and no one has said anything. At this point, you need to become a detective. Ask your rep to look into the situation; better yet, call the buyer yourself and "discover" what the problem is that everybody has swept under the rug—and promise to make immediate amends. Follow up and make sure that the little problem is taken care of before it again becomes an unmanageable albatross.

You discover general apathy among your salespeople and suspect lack of motivation.

1. It is time to study up on means of motivation. Personal pride and recognition opportunities for increased income (the "PPI Factor") are the prime ingredients of improved motivation.
2. Is it time for a general meeting or an intense motivational training session?

You know a problem exists with your staff, but everybody has clammed up and won't talk.

Make sure you have the confidence of every person on your sales team, and then ask each person to respond immediately and confidentially to your visit, call, or letter. The problem might be top management, or your people may be afraid to touch what is perceived as a "hot potato." Maybe they have found your product unsellable or uncompetitive but are loath to talk and jeopardize their jobs.

You recognize that changes are necessary, but you can't get through management to make those changes a reality.

It might be simple inertia—management's way of saying, "We've always done it this way."

1. Perhaps product redesign, a new credit policy, better service, repricing the line, and/or a change in marketing is the answer.

The Problem	A Possible Solution
	2. As a good salesperson, it might be up to you to "sell" your own company on your proposed changes and make a convincing proposal to the boss or the board.
Too many mistakes, too many returns, and too many process or quality problems are cutting into your income and that of your sales team, with subsequent unhappiness and dissatisfaction.	1. Pinpoint the specific areas of the complaints; document and measure them. 2. If they are outside of the sales team, meet with appropriate department heads. 3. If the problems are within your team, make special efforts to meet with the offender and attempt to conduct a coaching session. 4. If they are general mistakes, call a meeting to explore and implement corrections, such as retraining or, in extreme cases, replacing individuals.
It's hard to put your finger on the true cause, but you sense that morale is low, little "esprit de corps" exists, and sales are at a standstill or slipping.	It's time for a pep talk and some action. 1. Are you coaching each team member often enough? 2. Do your salespeople know that they are members of a team or do they think they are being ignored? 3. Is the merchandise or service becoming humdrum and non-competitive? 4. Is Rip van Winkle running the company? 5. How about a weekend get-together with families, a contest in which everyone could be a winner, or a game against another division of the company? How about a revitalized mission for the company or the sales force? What about product redesign or new products, a fresh campaign, a PR coup, or a major sales success story?

The Team Approach to Selling and Managing

The era of Willy Loman—the rugged individual, the pioneering loner—is over. What ever happened to Willy? He was the salesman of his day. His market research consisted of learning the newest joke, his "training" was sprints to the railroad station, and his education involved listening to lonely people in lonely bars. Willy never really was successful, but he managed to get by for a while—and then his sales began to drop. The further they dropped, the more Willy talked; he talked a little louder and a little longer, but it didn't help much.

Arthur Miller wrote the story of Willy's demise in his famous play *Death of a Salesman*. What did happen to Willy Loman? He was killed by a new society—a society which forced a change in a long-established method of doing business, a society which dramatically altered the roles of those who sell products and those who manage salespeople. It was a society to which poor Willy couldn't adjust.

Willy couldn't adjust because he couldn't even begin to understand or recognize what was taking place. Everything was too complex, and it was closing in all around him. There was nothing he could hold on to, and no one he could turn to for help. Willy sank deeper and deeper, and then he was dead. So, where does that bring us today?

The Willy Lomans have been replaced by a team. It is not always easy to adapt to the team concept. Once we are able to cast aside any inbred individualism (but certainly not our individuality) and get rid of jealousy and false superiority, we can begin to see that teamwork is the way to win the game.

Teamwork

In short, teamwork is:

- The ability to work together toward a common goal and vision
- The ability to direct individual accomplishments toward organizational objectives
- The fuel that allows ordinary people to attain extraordinary results

People in sales and sales management are learning that teamwork is more important today than in the past. Why? Because economic, cultural, political, environmental, and international changes are taking place at rocket speed. These changes are having an impact on organizations and individuals. *Teamwork* enables organizations to be more flexible, to respond quickly, and to adopt creative solutions to meet today's and tomorrow's challenges in an increasingly competitive environment.

Teamwork helps us reach goals more effectively. It increases the odds of the company doing the right thing at the right time—because there are many heads working on solutions. In essence, what teamwork does is eliminate internal competition and tensions and channel the group's energy toward cooperative achievement.

The team approach to selling did not develop overnight. The following trends have stimulated its current popularity in sales management:

- The success of the Japanese style of management, which stresses employee involvement in all phases of work
- Rejection of the old-style autocratic leadership by today's generation
- Rapid changes in technology that demand quick group response
- Emphasis on quality, which requires team efforts on an organizational scale
- Continuous information updating and learning

Rather than stifling the competitive spirit of organizations, team efforts can actually stimulate it and help organizations move forward. Lee Iaccoca on the industrial front and John F. Kennedy on the political front used teamwork to fine-tune their organizations. They started by picking the right team members; then they motivated them and trained them until they were in top shape. They developed plans, controls, and evaluation mechanisms as the organization developed.

According to the American Management Association:

> Teamwork means people cooperating to meet common goals. That includes all types of people doing work that calls for joint effort and exchange of information, ideas, and opinions. In teamwork, productivity is increased through synergy, the magic that appears when team members generate new ways for getting things done and that special spirit for getting them done.

When a Team Is Not Your Dream

Team building in sales management has become something of a buzzword. However, there is danger in thinking that all selling is improved by team selling. Teams do work splendidly most of the time, but there are also instances when individuals can be more effective or when the team is not yet ready to function effectively as a true team.

Because not all sales situations are alike, the first thing to decide is whether a team is the best way to organize your sales force. More often than not, it may be, but a team is not a cure-all.

The person who delivers goods to a customer a thousand miles away or the expert service technician who repairs malfunctioning computers is probably better off working on his or her own. The guard on a basketball team or the fire fighter battling a blaze can function only as a member of a team.

As the coach of a sales team, it is easy to fall into the common trap of being patronizing or even paternal. You need to coach your team members to play the game according to your rules, but also according to their abilities and skills. You, the coach, cannot control your sales reps. Once you let them go to work, they need to be free, unfettered, and responsible for their actions as individuals. The *teamwork* surfaces in your analysis of total results.

Ideally, a team should consist of members who all pull fairly equal loads. But what happens when the team includes an underachiever? The underachiever could be a holdover from a previous team or a relative who is "protected." While such a person often is known to be second-rate, management hopes that inclusion in an effective team will make this laggard perform up to speed.

Unfortunately, this kind of management optimism is not always warranted. The sales manager then has the ticklish task of trying to straighten out someone who could prove demoralizing to the other team members. He or she can do a coaching analysis, which attempts to get at the cause of unsatisfactory performance. The manager can then discuss the problems with the person, do some retraining and coaching, or suggest a transfer to another slot. If all else fails, the manager can go to top management with the problem to find a solution that is favorable for the company and the sales team.

Other obstacles to effective team operation might include:

- Playing politics
- Less-than-candid evaluation
- Back-stabbing or jealousy
- Lying
- Lack of information feedback
- Team-based compensation
- Cross-training/not enough shared responsibility

The experienced manager and team leader understands and even expects these obstacles. By expecting these human traits to surface occasionally, he or she is prepared for them with countermeasures.

Playing politics—Playing politics happens in every group activity, from a college class to an army platoon to a sales team. Maintaining a fair and impartial leadership role may be difficult, but it must be done because playing politics is a stumbling block to team effectiveness.

Less-than-candid evaluation—Dishonesty can pose an even more difficult problem. Sales figures and records are usually the best guide. However, since we are dealing with talented and ethical adults, the team leader should be able to rely on the team members' honesty to put all their cards on the table. As in a brainstorming session, only positive comments should be offered and only constructive contributions aired. Every team member needs to be trained as a diplomat. Have an "honesty meeting", so that the team can function smoothly and work toward the same company goal. Consider using the words of Chester Bowles, a prominent politician, journalist and national administrator of the Office of Price Administration during World War II: "Despite whatever agreement there may be between some of us, let us never forget that we are all working wholeheartedly for the same goal."

Lack of information feedback—One of the major gripes of employees is that they are not informed about company policy, product or service details, marketing plans, and competitive surprises. Total information feedback is important to the morale of the team; without it, any negative revelations picked up by team members in the field could have disastrous repercussions.

> Real communication goes in both directions...You have to be able to listen well if you're going to motivate the people who work for you.
>
> —Lee Iaccoca

Team-based compensation—Not giving every team member comparable compensation for joint efforts is also a shoal that has sundered many a team. Two advantages of team-based compensation are:

1. Management will avoid favoritism, which can hurt the effectiveness of a sales team.

2. Team members will soon learn that working together is the way to achieve individual gain. The French call this *esprit de corps,* and it can work wonders, though it is not a natural human instinct and needs to be developed.

Cross-training—Cross-training with other teams or individuals whose support is necessary for your sales team's success is also important. Such training could involve shipping clerks, delivery people and truckers, the credit department, buyers of supplies, and production line personnel. They all need to know that only through team efforts can they complete the cycle that provides the profit that pays their salaries. Any break in the cycle affects everyone.

Building a dream team is not easy or always possible—or even desirable. Does your situation warrant a team effort? Do you have the means, the time, and the overall understanding of how this can be achieved? The entire process is a developmental one, and it takes time and money, but when it works well, it can truly be a winning combination.

How to Set Up Satisfying Quotas

Setting up the right quotas for each player on your sales team is an excellent start toward building that dream team. It's like making projections for next year's budget. Professional salespeople usually like quotas because they are a challenge, like playing "Wheel of Fortune." Use the following four bases to create quotas:

First Base: What type of sales are you aiming for?

Second Base: Which markets are you targeting?

Third Base: Which products or services need to be promoted?

Home Plate: What profit goals are you aiming for?

Once you have established company goals, you need to match your quota projections with the actual situations and personnel at your disposal:

Territory—Can you estimate a realistic potential for the area assigned to the salesperson? You can't squeeze water out of a stone, so the assigned territory must have the potential to allow your quota to be reached.

History—If you have sold in the territory before, then you can use sales records as a pragmatic gauge. For a new territory, available demographics, market research, and personal explorations are called for to give you proper background data.

Human factor—What can you expect of the individual assigned to the territory? If you know the sales representative's strengths and prior performance, you can estimate his or her potential. Pinpoint the representative's strengths and use them to achieve optimum productivity.

Self-quotas—If you are blessed with a sales representative who suggests his or her own quota, listen carefully. If the rep is ambitious and wants to achieve more and his or her income has risen steadily, chances are the self-imposed quota will be both realistic and achievable. Such quotes are usually the result of personal challenges and field experience. Quotas can also be a great barometer for use by the home-office and helpful in planning factory production for the coming season.

Month-by-month quotas—More sales managers are using segmented, short-term quotas, because they are more predictable, more manageable, and easier to adjust. (This specific recommendation is also discussed later in this book.)

Seasonal variations—Many products and services are subject to strong sales variations during each season. Like Vivaldi's famed composition, sales curves are affected by fluctuating consumer demands. Many changes can affect quotas, and they should be taken into consideration so as to establish realistic and achievable quotas. Some of these changes include:

- Past performance statistics
- Local industrial and agricultural conditions
- Seasonal movement of consumers (Florida, for instance, has twice as many tourists during the winter months as the state's permanent population)

- Changes in dealer or distribution organization
- Availability of supplies and personnel
- Tax season, etc.

Existing market share—Territories must be analyzed for their current market share and potential. Some sales territories might be fairly saturated, whereas others have much additional potential for sales and still others have been barely touched. Each situation will determine the expansion quota.

Local economic conditions—Local economic factors are important influences. Long-term strikes, wild fluctuations in industrial production or crop production, shifts in consumer demands, and even recent natural disasters can cause dislocations in a local economy and adversely affect sales quotas. Sales reps cannot be expected to perform miracles.

Internal factors—While it is easy enough to establish statistical quotas, they have to be related to ability to perform. Product or personnel shortages, transportation difficulties, or corporate financing problems may mean that it is not be feasible to expand quotas.

Promotional campaigns—Companies "invest" (i.e., spend) varying percentages in advertising and sales promotion activities. These expenditures are true investments if they are made to increase business or improve the company's image. A major promotional campaign, either on a national scale or in a specific territory, demands an increase in quotas.

Technical dependency—If your product requires considerable engineering or other high-tech support, then the availability of such personnel and the time and cost needed for implementation must be considered. Quotas are meaningless if such technical support is not coordinated with them.

Delivery efficiency—The most annoying and counterproductive lapses that affect quotas are delayed delivery, improperly filled orders, and faulty delivery. Once customers have made the decision to buy, they want the goods or services yesterday. The salesperson must therefore establish the delivery times and conditions, and the shipping department must honor those commitments made in the field. Often the shipping department does not recognize the importance of its function in the sales chain. Quotas are impossible to fulfill if this link in the chain works inefficiently. It can mean missed quotas and can ruin the entire sales process.

Credit crunch—It is almost a tradition in companies that the sales department sells and the credit department unsells. Of course, it is necessary for customers to pay their bills within a reasonable and agreed-upon period of time. The credit policy should be clearly established, known to the sales representative, and passed on to the customer. If there is any doubt that the customer can pay on time, other arrangements for delayed billing or factoring should be activated. There is little purpose in establishing expanded quotas if the customer does not have the ability to pay for the goods or services. Today, creative financing is part of the salesperson's bag of tricks. Without it, company or individual quotas are meaningless.

Coaching Performance Test

The hands-on sales manager of the 1990s is increasingly assuming the role of coach for the team rather than just being an administrator. The functions demanded of the sales manager include trainer, problem solver, forecaster, motivator, parental figure, psychologist, and shrewd marketer—all rolled into one. The purpose of the test on the next page is to:

1. Identify the sales manager's strengths
2. Focus on areas for improvements
3. Determine specific training development skills

There are three ways in which this can be done:

1. Sales managers can use this checklist/test to evaluate their own performance, providing they feel comfortable with this objective approach.
2. The vice president of sales or the company president can use his test to monitor their various sales managers, i.e., regional, district, or specific product line.
3. Training directors can administer and evaluate the test and assess further training needs.

Coaching Performance Test

Manager/Coach_____

Salesperson coached_____

Date_____   Time_____

Rating scale: 0 = did not observe, 1 = unsatisfactory, 2 = needs improvement, 3 = satisfactory, 4 = above average, 5 = superior

Overall Coaching Skills

Establishes an attitude of trust	0	1	2	3	4	5
Performance versus standards evaluation	0	1	2	3	4	5
Explains the reason for this coaching	0	1	2	3	4	5
Maintains a positive atmosphere	0	1	2	3	4	5
Keeps discussion on track at all times	0	1	2	3	4	5
Encourages free exchange of ideas and feelings	0	1	2	3	4	5
Probes for sufficient detail	0	1	2	3	4	5
Listens without interruption	0	1	2	3	4	5
Observes and analyzes performance	0	1	2	3	4	5

Offering Quality Feedback

Offers positive comments about performance	0	1	2	3	4	5
Encourages focus on positive behavior	0	1	2	3	4	5
Asks salespeople what changes they made in their selling behavior and why	0	1	2	3	4	5
Offers other positive observations about salesperson performance	0	1	2	3	4	5
Expresses confidence about salesperson	0	1	2	3	4	5
Summarizes feedback discussion	0	1	2	3	4	5
Sells salesperson on need to change	0	1	2	3	4	5

Problem Solving

Admits that performance problems exist	0	1	2	3	4	5
Reviews possible solutions	0	1	2	3	4	5
Asks salesperson what specific action he or she will take	0	1	2	3	4	5
Agrees on specific actions and sets timetable	0	1	2	3	4	5
Reviews and confirms understanding of actions	0	1	2	3	4	5
Expresses confidence in salesperson	0	1	2	3	4	5
Summarizes problem-solving discussion	0	1	2	3	4	5
Follows up on how salespeople develop	0	1	2	3	4	5
Overall Rating	0	1	2	3	4	5

Notes for coaching the sales manager:_____

_____

_____

Selling the "Big Q" in Your Coaching and Training

The "Big Q" is *Quality*. Quality is not a recent discovery; it is a tried-and-true ingredient in companies that want to be proud of their products and services—and want to stay in business.

The late Dr. Deming persuaded the Japanese to move away from the global image of their products as cheap imitations and instead concentrate on quality products. Quality training gurus like Phil Crosby have built entire careers on the premise that quality does not cost—it pays.

This is certainly nothing new. H.J. Heinz preached quality well before World War II. He was selling a can of tomatoes for 12 cents when most of his competitors only asked a dime.

Some of his salesmen thought that if Heinz put out a cheaper brand, they would have an easier time selling their products. "Don't you know," old man Heinz told them, "that the reason this business has been successful is because we don't have a 10-cent can to sell? We don't want to put ourselves in the 10-cent class. Sell quality and the price won't matter."

Consider a Steinway piano. It sells for considerably more than most other pianos, yet Steinway's sales have been well above those of its competitors for decades. The quality image of Steinway is obviously worth millions.

The quality image can also be seen in clothing. Over 50 years ago, Knox was a high quality brand of hats. Supreme Court Justice Louis Brandeis was once asked by a market researcher why he preferred wearing only Knox hats. "I am quite aware that I am paying more for a Knox hat," Justice Brandeis said, "but the feeling that I am wearing a Knox hat is worth the difference."

Many goods are built down to a price rather than up to a standard. That's okay, because there will always be people who buy based on price alone and others who insist on quality. Over the past decade, many stores have traded up to quality merchandise while other retailers have emphasized lower priced or discounted merchandise. There is room for everyone, but two old adages still hold true: "Every man knows his worth" and "You get only what you pay for."

A couple of generations ago, the Dartnell Corporation stated that the customer "who buys a quality product soon forgets that he paid more for it, and remembers only the satisfaction it gives him…Quality is the strongest talking point a salesperson can have…Quality means repeat orders. It means trade that stays with you year in and year out. It means that you will be able to hold what you have and add to it. In short, it means enduring success, and not success built upon the quicksand of here-today-gone-tomorrow customers."

A woman comes into a store to look at a fur coat. The coat she has in mind sells for somewhat under $1,000. The salesperson lifts a beautiful mink coat out of the display rack and says, "Let's try this one on and see how it fits." Of course, it fits beautifully and looks stunning. "Turn around and see how it looks from the back," the salesperson urges. The customer breaks out in a smile.

The coat costs more than twice as much as what the customer had in mind, but the salesperson continues: "This is a coat that all your friends will oooh and ahhh over. Actually, when you consider that it is a lifetime purchase, it costs no more than a less expensive coat." Then she proceeds to tell the customer the cost of the other coat would be the down payment on the more expensive one and that the balance could be paid off over a one- to three-year period—while the customer enjoys wearing it.

When the customer hesitates, the salesperson throws in, "What we'll do is put this beautiful mink coat in our winter storage during your payoff period—at no charge." The coat is sold. Selling quality is not what it is, but what it does!

Framing the Picture

I recently visited an art gallery and was given four large postcards that depicted four of the fine artists represented by the gallery. Shortly thereafter, I was in a store that had a sale on simple but attractive frames. I bought four of them and mounted the four colorful postcards in them and then hung all four on a wall as a grouping.

Numerous people have commented on this handsome display, thinking they probably sold for $75 to $100 each. My cost was under $12 for all of them. It was proper packaging that made the product look so good.

The same can be said for selling perfume or jewelry—or selling yourself. "You don't have to be a millionaire to look like one," said a sales trainer more than five decades ago.

The point is that if you want to sell a quality product or service, you have to look *quality*. It is not necessary to wear a $500 suit, but make sure that whatever suit you wear is well-pressed.

When you put your best foot forward, make sure it is well shined! When you make a sales call, remember that you are the company in the customer's eyes.

Quality Means Selling Results

A man was having his dream house built, an elegant townhouse in the suburbs of his city. The price was just over $250,000, and each phase of the construction led to a meeting between him and his contractor.

The standard hardware cost about $1,000, but the superior type, from a maker that assured lifetime quality, came to a whopping $3,000. The owner's budget seemed stretched already, but the contractor said, "The cost of the best hardware, which immediately marks the house as a superior home, is only one percent of the total cost. I believe that you will get more than that back if you ever decide to sell the house. Meanwhile, you can enjoy the beauty of the best."

The owner bought the quality hardware. It only came to about $10 more a month, but it gave the home a million dollars worth of superiority.

The contractor was selling benefits—results—not price. He, too, benefited by being able to show others the fine home he had built. The contractor's pride in his achievement, and in his customer's satisfaction, also lasted forever.

Would the customer come back? Only to offer praises and with recommendations to other customers. Discounts are kept quiet; pride and results are talked about.

A Closing Quote on Quality

Half a century ago, a wise man named J.C. Aspley wrote:

> Above all, hold fast to your faith in quality. It is the rock upon which most businesses that have endured the years are built. It is the rock upon which the successful careers of thousands of top-flight salespeople have been founded. It has weathered depressions, booms, and busts. Twice blessed is the salesperson who has a quality product and or quality service to sell and knows how to sell it.

Summary of Key Ideas

What Is Coaching and Why Should You Develop the Skill?

Coaching is a face-to-face process to help you analyze and improve the performance of the sales staff you manage. You must do more than motivate if you want to improve performance. You must reinforce good behavior and show your salespeople how to correct their own behavior problems.

You cannot correct behavior by talking in generalities (e.g., "Shape up—you have a lousy attitude"). Too often, managers are taught what they should do instead of how to do it. You are judged as a manager by the performance of the salespeople you manage. Any time you choose not to help your salespeople improve, you are involved in self-destructive behavior.

Consider three basic facts about sales management:

1. Management is getting things done through others.
2. You need your salespeople more than they need you.
3. You get paid for what your salespeople do, not what you do.

Your role is to provide the game plan and to do everything in your power to help your salespeople be successful, so the team can be successful.

Too often, field sales managers try to change their salespeople rather than change their behavior. In *Coaching for Improved Sales Performance,* Ferdinand Fournies states that salespeople or district managers have what he terms a "behavior rental agreement":

1. A district manager has no right to change a salesperson.
2. A district manager does have a right, and responsibility, to try to change or improve an employee's behavior if that person isn't behaving as he or she agreed to behave.

Fournies says, "Deal with behavior, not people. You can see behavior, measure it, talk about it unemotionally. You can also change it."

Turnover of salespeople is a costly process in terms of both time and money. It is far more economical to improve a person's performance than it is to replace that person.

Sometimes a customer is like a cow. A cow does not give milk. You've got to take it from her twice a day—otherwise she won't give any moo-lah!

—Joe Weldon

The 5 Most Important Words...

The FIVE most important words: You did a good job
The FOUR most important words: What is your opinion?
The THREE most important words: Can I help?
The TWO most important words: Thank you.
The ONE most important word: You.
(The least important word: I)

—Author unknown

The best coaches set in motion a continuing learning process—that, we find, helps people develop a tolerance for their own struggles and accelerates the unfolding of skill and contributions that would not have been possible without the "magic" attention of a dedicated coach.

—Nancy Austen and Tom Peters
A Passion for Excellence

Effective coaching requires a balanced discussion in which the leader first tries to understand before he or she tries to be understood.

—Steven J. Stowell
Training & Development Journal

1. The coach should care about the people under his guidance.
2. He should decide how best to use his personnel and then have the ability to teach.
3. It is important to motivate each individual to work to the best of his ability.

—Dean Smith, University of North Carolina

Coaching Visit—Planning Worksheet

Sales Rep. To Be Coached:_____

Review Past Sales Performance History:

Analyze Current Sales Results:

Review Possible Causes of Variances:*

Priorities for This Visit:

Arrange Visit (specific accounts, type of accounts, specific product(s), areas, type of calls, itinerary):

* Variance is any departure from plan or projections. A variance can be positive (e.g., sales X percent higher than quota) or negative (e.g., failure to follow itinerary).

CHAPTER 8

Secret #7: Motivation—Key to Excellence

> You don't motivate people to succeed, instead you provide
> people with an opportunity to succeed and *they* will become
> motivated.
>
> —Herzberg

A generation ago, when I was an undergraduate taking a course in basic psychology, the professor called my attention to a man named Ernest Dichter. He was called "the Father of Motivation."

Dr. Dichter impressed me to no end. He was the first person to put Mrs. Consumer on the couch and psychoanalyze her, looking for deep-down reasons for purchasing one product rather than another. Some of the biggest companies of the day, many of which are still around, were Dr. Dichter's clients.

Motivation remains a viable concept, which is why it is one of the "secrets" to success. It was discussed as far back as the 19th century, although it wasn't called motivation. More than 100 years ago, English historian and critic John Ruskin expressed it as follows:

> In order that people may be happy in their work, these three
> things are needed: they must be for it; they must not do too
> much of it; and they must have a sense of success in it.

In other words, to get your staff to perform at an optimum level:

- They must be convinced it's a good thing.
- They must realize that too much of even a good thing can be unhealthy ("the burnout syndrome").
- They must see that rewards come to those who work hard.

Self-Motivation

Many years ago, I heard a speaker say: "There is some bad news and some good news about motivation. The bad news is that you can't motivate anybody; all motivation is self-motivation. The good news is that the only motivation that is really effective is self-motivation." Your primary job as a sales manager is to create an environment in which your salespeople will motivate themselves. They will change their thinking about getting the sales job done from "have to" to "want to."

Our "wants" are great motivators. It might take a little digging, but if you can discover what each of your salespeople *wants,* then you will have him or her working hard to achieve it. And don't worry that once those wants are fulfilled the salesperson will lay down on the job.

Several decades ago, American management expert Douglas McGregor said: "Man is a wanting animal. As soon as one of his needs is satisfied, another appears in its place. This process is unending. It continues from birth to death."

Of course, wants have cultural components. A few years ago, a big rebuilding program was progressing in St. Croix, one of the U.S. Virgin Islands. A stateside contractor set up a business to build new homes and rebuild others that had been devastated by a hurricane on the island.

The contractor was pleased when his crew performed exceptionally well. At the end of the fourth week, he gave the supervisor a sizable bonus as an incentive to complete the second half of the building job. It was a Friday afternoon, and the crew was to begin again early Monday morning.

On Monday morning, most of the crew showed up, but the supervisor was not among them. The puzzle continued right into Tuesday, when the man arrived with a big smile and no apologies. The contractor asked why he had neither shown up nor let him know that he wouldn't be there. The supervisor said matter-of-factly, "Why, boss, you paid me for Monday ahead of time, and it was such a good day, I just went fishing."

So much for the McGregor principle of continuing wants. Each person has a ceiling of ambition, and it is the sales manager's job to discover how high it is.

Sometimes the most effective motivation is a veiled or real threat. When the San Francisco Giants baseball team was lagging badly, manager Dave Bristol felt he needed to do something to spark more spirit in his men. On the morning of the next big game, he called the men together and said: "There'll be two busses leaving the hotel for the ballpark. The two o'clock bus will be for those of you who need a little extra work. The empty bus will be leaving at five o'clock."

Dichter Dictum

The human brain operates at about 15 percent of capacity, and the body at 40 to 50 percent of capacity. One of the most effective ways to motivate others and ourselves is to encourage the use of some of our reserve potential.

To successfully motivate others, good managers must possess three qualities:

1. **The ability to bring out the best in co-workers**—While *adaptation, critiques, and compliments play important* roles, leaders can make people feel good about themselves and help them gain self-esteem. Leaders who don't flaunt their own egos become the best motivators.

2. **The courage to break new ground**—Leaders need to ask *why,* to create new approaches within the organization, and to develop new products and processes.

3. **Consistency in planning and reliability of performance**—Employees need to know where you want them to go; they shouldn't be left wondering. Uncertainty breeds confusion, unhappiness, and insecurity.

When orders and policies are confusing or contradictory, employees lose their motivation. Clear, unequivocal communication avoids confusion. When this is absent, it might be the manager or supervisor's fault. See if any of the following occurred:

1. The sales manager or person in charge might have been too impatient.

2. The salesperson's ability to understand or to follow orders might have been overestimated.

3. The sales manager and top management needed to prove their superiority and wanted to see the salesperson fail.

4. Orders or instructions were given in such a confusing way that failure was virtually inevitable. (Again, could the top manager's insecurity be at work?)

5. The sales manager was unsure of the objective or the means to reach it and unconsciously asked the staff for help and direction.

At this point, we are separating positive sales managers from negative sales managers. Ernest Dichter compares the latter to dictators. They take advantage of other people's confusion by fostering dependence, whereas positive leaders train people to act independently.

Others Involved in Motivation

Dichter was not alone in exploring motivation. Freud dabbled in it, focusing on emotions and the irrationality of human drives. Behaviorist B.F. Skinner believed that human beings are completely trainable and are motivated through reinforcements, almost like Pavlov's dogs.

As practical sales managers, we don't have the time to delve into academic concerns. We know, however, that building motivation helps achievement and that motivation is created by setting clear, reachable goals for each and every sales representative.

Whatever the goals—money, awards, profit sharing, or recognition—they are the "green stamps" that will make a person work harder. The reps will come again and again until their little premium booklets are filled.

Dichter's Seven-Step Process

Dichter sees the achievement of proper motivation as a seven-step process:

Step 1: Self-knowledge—Encourage individuals to recognize their own abilities and weaknesses; talk about how these abilities are changing. How do they as individuals influence progress within the organization and relationships among peers?

Step 2: Information handling/control of environment—Due to the rapidly changing nature of information, materials, and markets, new methods for storing and retrieving data need to be learned. Information should be readily accessible and helpful in generating new and innovative approaches.

Step 3: Personal organization—Moving up in the company hierarchy tends to isolate executives, keeping them out of touch with day-to-day reality. Many functions are indirect and often ceremonial. New priorities need to be set that classify information in functional rather than superficial ways. This is necessary in order to organize an increased workload.

Step 4: Dynamic technical communication—While external communication in the form of the old-fashioned letter are usually unavoidable, internal communication can be streamlined by utilizing new electronic devices such as e-mail and voice mail, which free up considerable executive time.

Step 5: Interpersonal relations—This means developing greater sensitivity, becoming an active listener, not making rash judgments, and forcing oneself to use all the senses in observing people and one's environment. These characteristics make for better relations and increase the effectiveness of an executive. A one-page questionnaire at the end of this chapter can be used to keep personal information on each of your staff members.

Step 6: More creative thinking—The modern executive has to make decisions, think problems through, and understand increasingly complex issues. Some human frailties can get in the way:

- Misinterpreting other people's explanations
- Generalizing
- Attaching "labels" because of lack of proper information
- Failure to ask insightful questions
- Arriving at the wrong conclusion because of prejudices

In many organizations, *creative thinking* is stymied by real or imagined conventions. Innovation, like entrepreneurship, involves taking calculated risks.

Step 7: Encouragement to grow—It is important for both you and everyone you supervise to feel they have room to *grow*. Most people operate at half or less than half of their capacity. "Being told and cajoled to use the other half of our potential is one of the most effective ways of motivating ourselves and others," Dr. Ernest Dichter wrote.

What motivates managers to do a better job for themselves and for those they manage?

- Responsibility
- Trust
- Being listened to
- Working in teams
- Recognition for ideas generated
- Knowing why you are important to the organization
- Flexible controls
- Clear directions
- Measurable goals (See Chapter 4)
- Knowledge (pertinent skills, training, information)
- Support (approval, encouragement, feedback)
- Readily available resources
- Communication from and to management and employees

Self-Esteem: The Key to Performance

While working on a book about how people could become more productive, British writer Arnold Bennett often heard his publisher boast about his secretary's remarkable efficiency. On a visit to the publisher's office, he asked the secretary for the secret of her efficiency. "It's not my secret," she replied, "it's his. Every time I do any job, no matter how insignificant, he praises me so extravagantly that I feel I must live up to it."

Building your sales staff's self-esteem can be accomplished in many ways. One obvious method is praising and recognizing excellent performance. Giving the salesperson more authority also helps. It is vital to train managers about motivation techniques.

> The opportunity for sales people to express their views and opinions, in itself, does not improve self-esteem. But when management *listens, and responds and acts* on what they hear, not only is self-esteem improved, but a new positive atmosphere is created. Morale and motivation increase significantly.
>
> —Dr. Richard Bagozzi
> Sloan School of Management, MIT

Self-Determination Fuels Motivation

Sales managers' success depends on their ability to achieve results through their salespeople. Motivation is the lubricant, but it works better when people want to do what they are told they should do.

Motivation must stir each person from within. The key to stirring people up is to understand them as individuals—to know what turns them on. Blanket theories do not apply to groups.

In the television program *All in the Family*, Archie Bunker thought he understood Polish people, blacks, women, cab drivers—whoever crossed his path. He had an opinion about everyone. "All *those* people are alike. Once you know one of 'em, you know all of 'em." We laughed at Archie's foibles and prejudices and sneered at the fallacy of lumping all people into categories.

In a way, we often do the same thing in sales management, even though we should know better. We know that we often waste a lot of time trying to fit round pegs into square holes, applying cookie-cutter solutions to all individuals.

But there is a solution. While we can't motivate everybody in the same way and push everyone toward the same goals, we *can* provide people with the *opportunity to succeed*. We can expose them to a climate in which they want to work. When people see advantages, they will *motivate themselves*. Management must realize that *the only motivation that truly works is self-motivation.*

When Training Is Not Enough, Motivate Yourself

Some sales management experts believe in self-help. These are probably the same people who believe in offering unemployed workers training rather than unemployment compensation. As an adage advises us, teach a man how to fish rather than feeding him the fish that others caught.

Art Sobczak, a newsletter editor and specialist in telephone selling techniques, believes in self-motivation. "Don't expect other people to motivate you. They can't," he says.

Sobczak believes that there is no easy way to accomplish anything worthwhile and no easy way to stay motivated. He emphasizes that "Motivation, requires the 'W' word: WORK!" It has to come from within, and he has formulated nine steps to help salespeople motivate themselves.

1. **Ask yourself this question: "Have I ever really been motivated on this job?"**—Sobczak says that being passionate about your job is like being married; you need to put some romance into your work, just as you would with a relationship that has lost its spark.

2. **Have a mission**—Have one or more goals. Be focused. If you are focused on your destination, excitement and enthusiasm are natural by-products. Setting effective goals and then achieving them can be one of the most powerful tools in self-motivation (Learn how to do it the SMART way in Chapter 4.)

3. **Do things differently**—"The only way you'll ever get different results is to change your behavior," says Art Sobczak. He suggests that you "stretch a little, try new things, take some risks...determine what you could change for the better, and then do it!"

4. **Doubt your limitations**—Stop believing that just because something was done a certain way in the past, it must always be done that way. Don't be afraid to do something new just because you haven't done it before. Challenge yourself to do more, to do better. Old beliefs can become straightjackets to your success.

5. **Learn from every sales call**—Take a moment after every call to reflect, because learning takes place after doing an activity. "...Invest a few moments reacting to the experience, burning it into your mind, thinking about what you'll do the next time," Sobczak suggests.

6. **Add more knowledge to your frame of reference**—Practice does not make perfect; *perfect* practice makes perfect. Review some familiar inspirational motivation books or tapes. This second time through, the information might be even better because you have grown and developed. A great time to learn new things is while you are driving or traveling on a plane.

7. **Failure is consistent with achievement**—Be like a baby learning to walk—try, fall, get up, try, fall, get up. Eventually the baby learns to walk. As the Sinatra song says, when you fall down, "pick yourself up, dust yourself off, and start all over again." This is the true entrepreneurial spirit. It is said that each entrepreneur's success is preceded by 3.8 failures. As a rich old man said to his young admirers, "Yes, I am an instant success after 50 years of trying." Strength, determination, and smarts develop from failure and from trying again.

8. **Keep in mind whom you work for**—This is an easy test: look in the mirror. It's *you,* and you are the most important person in your world. Don't depend on others, because you are the captain of your own destiny. When grandmother was asked about the flavor of her chicken soup, she said: You put good things in; you get good things out. So it is with you. Your output is the direct result of your input.

9. **Take action**—Read the words in this book, all of them. Then *do* something about them. If you read the words but take no action, they are just so many symbols and not worth the paper they are printed on. The bottom line of this training lesson is: *do* it!

Motivation Training Doesn't Cost—It Pays

According to *Management Dimensions'* Robert J. Calvin, there are at least half a dozen good reasons why a sales training program that emphasizes motivational techniques is a good investment for any company:

- Salespeople are an expensive human resource, but *motivated* salespeople produce more dollars of revenue per dollar of expense.
- Motivated salespeople stay with you longer because they have less reason to leave (they simply make more money!), thus reducing the high cost of turnover.
- Motivating salespeople is especially important in small companies because of the limited career ladders and often limited remuneration.
- Motivated salespeople are not satisfied with giving a day's work for a day's pay: They want to give you a day-and-a-half's work for a day's pay.
- Motivation converts salespeople's complacency into enthusiasm.
- A motivated sales force costs no more than an unmotivated sales force. Why not have the best?

Tom Peters on Motivation

American management guru Tom Peters highlights three ingredients:

1. Be specific
2. Reinforce immediately
3. Make the mechanism achievable

In getting optimum value out of motivation, rewards should be unpredictable and intermittently used as reinforcement. If the recipient comes to expect rewards, then they lose their glamour. Big bonuses to a select few often become political and tend to discourage the majority of employees. The right kind of motivation, says Peters, satisfies "the insatiable human need to enhance one's self-image."

Peters' trademark is his frankness. He says: "I relish telling managers that they are first-class jerks if they don't listen to their employees, then act on what they hear..."

Tom Peters has long championed employee involvement, often referred to as *empowerment*. "The world would be a better place if we thanked employees more often for a job well done," Peters said referring to MCI, which he described as truly action-oriented, anti-bureaucratic, and disrespectful of job boundaries. One of MCI's chiefs, Dick Liebhaber, said, "We don't shoot people who make mistakes, we shoot people who don't take risks."

Peters also says that CNN motivates people to reach beyond self-imposed limitations. It is an action-oriented, empowered, spirited company, whose president, Burt Reinhardt, said, "Doing it means figuring out how to do it yourself. If your way works out most of the time, you'll get promoted."

General Electric's boss, Jack Welch, also addressed his managers by saying: "I want to tap the brains of *all* employees—if you can't do that, catch the next train out of town."

Peters believes that managers who do not empower employees to "tap their imagination and curiosity" will fall in the viciously competitive 1990s.

Employee Retention: Keeping Effective Salespeople Can Be the Ultimate Cost Saver

Looking for, hiring, and training new salespeople is a costly and time-consuming task. It consumes an inordinate amount of a sales manager's time. Consider the following costs for just one employee:

- Recruitment advertising
- Personnel agency fee
- Orientation
- Training
- Below-par sales results until new employee produces up to par

The total could easily be $5,000 or more.

Retaining a productive salesperson is always a smart investment. Over the past decade, many writers have discussed the ingredients that attract good people to companies and make them stay there. Of course, making money is one of the primary motivators, but "psychic income" has become more and more important to today's generation of sales professionals.

Such terms as benefits, trust, pride, freedom, fairness, fun, and a family atmosphere have been mentioned as reasons for employee loyalty and retention. Sometimes a company's accomplishments in such subjective areas as environmental concerns and business ethics contribute to employee pride.

Avoiding company politics and promoting based on on merit rather than favoritism might be difficult for the CEO and sales manager. However, he or she must strictly adhere to this principle.

Ways to Retain Employees

- Be patient and consistent in *your own behavior*; you are a role model.
- The *learning process* is merciless in revealing mistakes, both yours and those others make. Recognize mistakes and regard them as stepping-stones to improvement.
- *People come first.* Help them feel good about themselves. If they do something well, boost their self-esteem with some recognition.
- *Look at learning as a lifelong job.* Lifelong learning is the only way to remain competitive in the job market. Give your employees and trainees the incentive to invest in their own growth, development, and self-renewal. Learning is never costly; only ignorance is.
- *Communication* is always important. It is the only way others will know what you and the company want. Make consistent use of meetings, newsletters, suggestion boxes, and reward systems.

- *Promotion and recognition* of superior achievement are always needed. Wherever possible, look to promote from within and keep yourself apprised of the career goals of those working for you.
- Retain some *flexibility* in the job, and consider employees' family matters, personal interests, and aspirations.
- A safe and attractive *working environment* helps to ensure retention.
- Always bear in mind that employees also have personal lives. They own homes, send kids to college, and are concerned about healthcare coverage. When a company offers benefits in these areas, employees can concentrate on corporate tasks.
- *Recognition* needs to be reemphasized. Personal pride or ego rewards along with adequate income and security are the most important concerns of employees.

> If I am not for myself, who will be for me?
> If I am for myself, who am I?
> If not now, when?
>
> —Hillel, first century

Personal Information

Employee's Name_____

Home Address_____

Home Phone_____ E-Mail Address_____

Nickname_____ Age_____ Place of Birth_____

Length of Time with Company_____

Previous Jobs_____

Education_____

Professional Experience_____

_____

Memberships_____

Religion/Church_____

Polital Affiliation/Beliefs_____

Interests in Sports_____

Hobbies, Other Interests_____

_____

Smoking/Drinking Habits_____

Favorite Restaurants_____

Family Information: Spouse's Name_____

Children: Ages, Activities, Interests_____

_____

_____

Short-Range Professional Goals_____

Long-Range Professional Goals_____

Areas of Major Interest_____

_____

How He/She views Job and Business_____

_____

How He/She views Products/Services_____

_____

Additional Information_____

_____

_____

_____

_____

_____

_____

_____

Part II

Living the Seven Secrets

CHAPTER 9

Sizzlemanship—The Elmer Wheeler Story

One day more than 50 years ago, Elmer Wheeler, his era's most famous sales representative, rushed out of a hotel in Mexico, on his way to a meeting in another hotel. A man held out a single gardenia to him and implored, "Señor, buy this flower—it will make you look important all day!"

As Elmer told the story, he almost twisted his ankle making an about-face, as the full significance of the flower vendor's sentence struck him. "I had several important calls to make that day," Elmer said, "and that little man's sales pitch hit the nail squarely on the head—I did want to stand out, I did want to feel important, and I wanted this fragrant attention-getter to last all day. What a sales pitch in a few words!" He took 50 centavos out of his pocket and stuck the flower in his lapel.

Latin Americans sell with more emotion, more romance. The further north you go, the more logic creeps into the selling process. The ideal is, of course, a combination of the head and the heart.

Another example of "southern selling" that displayed true Wheeler "sizzlemanship" was his report from a trip to Havana, Cuba, in the pre-Castro days. As the ship docked and passengers stood in the immigration line on the dock, little boys would sidle up to each passenger, offering picture postcards of Cuba. The boys had already pasted the proper postage on the cards, saving the tourist the irritating task of finding stamps and thus eliminating any excuse for not buying.

To finalize the sale, the boys had pencils ready and said, "Let your friends know you are in Cuba. Here is a pencil." "Like any good tourist,"

Elmer Wheeler said, "I bought ten cards and paid in hard U.S. dollars—which is just what the little rascals wanted. But, it sure saved me time and possible inertia."

Make It Easy for the Customer to Buy!

Sell the benefits, motivate the buyer, and anticipate how to overcome a "no." Elmer Wheeler taught these and many other basic principles at his sales meetings and seminars. Most of them are so loaded with logic and common sense that one wonders why one never thought of them before.

Most selling involves new products or lines of products. Psychologists tell us not to take a phobia, neurosis, or hang-up away from people without offering an acceptable substitute. Similarly, if you sell a product that is designed to replace one the customer already has, you better have a string of good reasons why your product or service is better. *Always have a substitute ready to replace what you plan to take away!*

It is human nature to hesitate before making a decision. Expect that your prospect will question your offer, may say no, or at best, will demur and say he or she needs more time or must talk your offer over with whoever comes in handy as an alibi. It is therefore absolutely necessary that you anticipate what objections your prospect might come up with and prepare your sales presentation to overcome the negatives. *Plan your sales presentation in advance, and you will always be ahead of your prospect!*

There are several other secrets of salesmanship that Elmer Wheeler enunciated. They worked 50 years ago and no doubt work today. Human nature hasn't changed in the last few hundred years and certainly hasn't changed since the 1940s.

- Elmer Wheeler was a born psychologist. He had a knack, an instinct, and an ear and an eye for what sold. What made Wheeler's "sizzlemanship" so successful is that he accentuated the positive. As a pop tune in Wheeler's day advised: "Accentuate the positive...eliminate the negative." It pays to listen to popular lyrics; they contain much practical folk wisdom.

- One thing Wheeler made clear in giving us a heritage of great examples is not to give an undecided or indecisive customer too much latitude. Be positive and make your suggestions firm and specific. For example:

Don't say:	*Do say:*
What color do you want?	These are the season's newest colors.
Do you like red?	Blue is very much "in" this season.
May I help you?	Isn't this a great new style?
Shall I wrap it for you?	Please step over to the desk, and I'll be glad to wrap it for you.
Is there something for you?	These are the latest styles—they just came in.

If you want to get the right answer, you don't always have to ask the right question. Make an appropriate positive statement.

- In a way, Elmer Wheeler had the same sort of instinct, or perhaps technique, that many people have come to admire in H. Ross Perot. Nineteen percent of all American voters agreed in the November 1992 polls. Ross Perot believed in the power of words.

- As Wheeler put it: "Words that are slick, smart-sounding, or smart-aleck attract attention to themselves—not to the ideas or merchandise they are supposed to be presenting."

- He dramatized his conclusion by saying that no gun hits a target if it has blank cartridges. You need words that have meaning, that contain benefits, that sizzle. For example, "You don't have to buy this computer to get rid of me—but you do have to buy it to improve the efficiency and profit of your business.

- "Tune your sales talk into the other fellow's wavelength—get in step with him" is another of Wheeler's tried-and-tested maxims. To be on the same wavelength, you must get to know your prospects or customers.
  - What are their hobbies or interests?
  - What are convenient appointment times?
  - Have you prepared them to listen to how your product or service will accomplish their aims?
  - Are you using the words—the convincing arguments—that have been tested in previous sales battles?

If you have all this ammunition, you are in step with your customer.

Make It Easy for Them to Buy!

Sports lingo and examples were a favorite of Wheeler's, just as they are with many sales professionals and their customers. If you know your customers are golfers, show them how your product might lower their score. If they play tennis, tell them they can hardly miss with your oversize racket.

Get in step with the sports enthusiasts with an appropriate story or anecdote, and then let them open up and tell their "big fish" story to you. Most sports enthusiasts are loaded with stories they are anxious to tell. Elmer Wheeler counsels us to listen, and we will soon discover people's ambitions and secret desires.

The way you say something is as important as what you say. *The words that cause a dog to greet you with a friendly wag of his tail when you say them with a smile can cause him to slink away when you say them with a bark.*

Wheeler was also a great believer in *tactile selling*—touch, smell, and hold what you have to sell. It's the "monkey see, monkey do" instinct, as Elmer put it, and it's in every one of us. You can begin your presentation by demonstrating this tactile technique and then letting customers take their turn doing likewise. Seeing may be believing, but touching is convincing. "The clever sales rep knows that proof makes people buy faster than anything else," Wheeler said. You might say it with sizzle—but you sell it with proof!

While facts are necessary, especially in today's era of high-tech products and services that Wheeler never even dreamt of, his advice still holds true: One emotional thrill takes the place of a dozen logical facts!

When Wheeler was a space salesman in the advertising department of a Baltimore newspaper, he discovered that selling space got him nowhere, but keeping a *results* book for his advertisers measurably increased his sales. He showed his advertisers, item by item, what it cost them to advertise. Superior results produced much repeat advertising and commissions for the young Elmer Wheeler.

While the newspaper Wheeler represented was not the leading one, he and at least two of his followers who came on board after his departure produced consistently high returns and earnings. Wheeler developed a personal formula from this experience:

> Regardless of what business you are in, make the sizzle, the emotional sized, at least 75 percent of your sales effort. Let the other 25 percent be logical facts and arguments.

Wheeler developed developed another truism while at the runner-up newspaper in Baltimore: *Do not ask "do you want" but which!*

By way of dramatization, Wheeler said that he learned to rough out, or have the newspaper's artist create, three sketches of an ad: a full page, a half page, and a quarter page. Each had pictures of the store's merchandise, its logo, and perhaps the picture of the owner or manager. Wheeler called on the customer and offered a choice of one of the three suggested ads.

Of course price was a determining factor, but as often as not the advertiser would say that the full page was too expensive and the quarter page was too insignificant—and then settled on the half-page format.

Years after Wheeler's departure from the newspaper, the sales manager used the same technique and taught it to two sales reps. Both of them retired most comfortably some 30 years later after highly successful careers as "Wheelermen."

Fear appeal is no longer a respectable emotional buzzword, but Wheeler found it useful in some limited applications. This motivation is, of course, built into all laws. There has to be some negative result from not doing something that should be done. If you don't have your oil checked every 6,000 miles and replace the filter every 12,000 miles, the implication is that your car's motor will suffer and wear out more quickly. Wheeler admits that mature judgment can overcome fear appeal, but he offers the following advice:

> What will happen if you *don't* do something
> is often as effective as what will happen if you do it.

Remember that it was fear that motivated the first cave dweller to train a watchdog to help protect his home!

Resourcefulness is another lesson from Elmer Wheeler. It is, like fear itself, a quality to be handled with some care. Astute sales reps watch for buying signals, such as proper interest and body language. They know when to stay with the customer and when to get off the track.

Wheeler tells the fable of an Irishman running down the track ahead of a moving train. All the while he is running, he is puffing, "If I can only reach that switch!" A farmer by the roadside, leaning on his hoe, shouts to the runner, "Why don't you just get off the track and let the darn train pass?"

The moral of the story is that the runner hadn't thought of that solution. He lacked resourcefulness, which surpasses any bag of tricks that salespeople might pull out of their hats.

It's easy to get a prospect's attention but difficult to close the sale. If you put a naked mannequin in the window, people will stop by and stare. You've gotten their attention. If you hire a good-looking man or women to pass out samples at a trade show, a lot of samples will be distributed. But how many suspects will these *tricks* turn into prospects? *Resourcefulness that is too clever only loses out in the long run!*

Elmer Wheeler advises that knowing when to make your sales call is a fine selling point to practice.

- Early in the morning, buyers might have a pile of mail on their desks that needs to be checked.
- From about 10:00 to 11:30 A.M. is usually a good time for appointments.
- By 11:30, prospects begin to feel hungry, and their minds are occupied by lunch plans, unless you can persuade them to let you take them to lunch.
- After lunch, let your prospects get resettled and get their work in order.
- Right before and right after a holiday or a trip are bad times to schedule a call.
- Saturday mornings and Monday mornings are usually not favorable, unless customers request those times.
- Rainy days are good, because customers usually postpone going out.

Just as it is important to know when to make sales calls, it is important to know when to leave. You don't want the customer to avoid you on the next call. *Be the first to end the interview.*

Elmer Wheeler's "sentences that sizzle" were the topic of many sales sessions in famous companies. He compiled about a thousand of such sentences. In the days when salespeople considered $25 a week good pay, Wheeler was charging from $1,000 to $4,000 for one of his famed sizzlemanship training sessions. Often, when we think we have created a particularly effective truism about a sales situation, we are in effect repeating one of Wheeler's truisms.

Just as photocopies have become "Xerox" copies and tissues have become "Kleenex," Elmer Wheeler's "sizzling sentences" are part of the folklore of the sales profession. One reason they have lasted and remained effective is that they are so basic. They go to the emotions, to the psychology, of human beings, and we need to remember and practice them.

Here are a handful of Wheeler's best proverbs:

- Ask the right question, and you'll get the right answer.
- It's not what a product or service costs, but what it may save the customer that counts.
- Time your entrance—and your exit.
- Gain your prospect's confidence—it makes the sale.
- Compare the unknown with the known—the things people don't understand with the things they do understand.
- Direct your sales talk to the prospect's emotions—not his reason. It's the emotional appeal that makes the sale.
- Plan your sales presentation in advance, and you'll always be ahead of your prospect.

Professors Are Always Right!

At the height of his career, supersalesman Elmer Wheeler was voted "America's Number One Public Speaker" by a poll of 500 business clubs. However, as a college student, he failed a public speaking course. His professor told him that he should find a profession in which he would not come into contact with the public. At his peak, Wheeler addressed more than a million people a year.

CHAPTER 10

Time Management

Lost, yesterday, somewhere between sunrise and sunset, two golden hours, each set with 60 diamond minutes; no reward is offered for they are gone forever.

—Horace Mann, 1796–1859

Time is the most paradoxical element in our lives. Either we have all the time in the world, or we never have enough of it. We can waste time or continually run out of it. One thing is certain: we can't go to the store and buy time, even though we may use that expression to mean we are putting off a decision or an inevitable conclusion.

Time is the element by which we measure our progress. We translate time into monetary worth when we achieve a task within a certain time frame and calculate a cost-per-hour figure. Tradesmen work by the hour more than sales executives do, but the latter's time is equally valuable, even if not as strictly accounted for.

Time is a very elastic concept. If it takes you two hours to go to customer's place of business, make a presentation, and get back to your hotel, office, or car to process the order, you tend to figure out how much money you made and how much it comes out to by the hour. But is this *all* the time you spent in making the sale?

Four Rules for Maximizing Your Use of Time

The most successful managers of the late 1990s and into the 21st century will follow four basic rules for maximizing their time:

1. **Develop purpose statements**—The first step in maximizing the personal and organizational use of time is the development of an organizational and a personal mission or purpose statement. This clarifies one's purpose and values, and sets priorities prior to setting objectives.

2. **Set priorities**—According to Stephen Covey in his book *First Things First*, most time management tools focus on prioritizing and accomplishing such urgent activities as crises, pressing problems, deadline-driven projects, interruptions, and some meetings. You can't do everything all at once. Focusing on the "important" but not the "urgent" activity makes the vital difference in maximizing your use of time. In the sales profession, the first priority is to deal with issues that have the potential to produce profit or increase sales. Expense items, such as monitoring and managing the budget that influences profit, might be the next priority One sales manager prioritizes his tasks as follows:
   a. Coaching those "B" salespeople who could become "A's"
   b. Planning "A" account visits with their account executive
   c. Strategic market planning

3. **Delegate**—This can often be difficult, especially for rugged individualists and entrepreneurs. Look at your tasks and decide if someone else can initiate or complete them. The essence of good management is to delegate as many jobs as possible. Concentrate on those jobs in which you excel; let somebody else do those you find too difficult, a pain in the neck, or which require too much research on subjects with which someone else might already be familiar. In today's era of team playing, delegating some tasks will make your team members feel good and encourage them to try harder.

4. **Agendas**—These are crucial, especially during meetings. No meeting should be conducted without an agenda. An agenda explains, better than most tools, the company or department's priorities and objectives. (A Meeting-Agenda form at the end of this section can be used to build an agenda.) It is also important to start and end meetings on time. After all, time is what this chapter is all about.

Here are a couple of additional pointers:

- **Interruptions**—Some are inevitable. The smart manager is realistic and allows for interruptions by not scheduling work or activity segments too tightly. We often think that we are superhuman and try to do too many things in too short a time frame. A phone call, an emergency visit from a staff member, an interview, and a call to see the boss right away are all inevitable interruptions. Like unexpected expenses in pricing products and services, you need to account for unplanned interruptions in your time schedule. If you don't, you'll drive yourself crazy.

- **Procrastination**—Of course, this does not apply to *you,* but it is nevertheless important to mention. Procrastination is an insidious enemy of time. It is usually caused by fear or disinterest, and it takes a lot of discipline to overcome. One way to overcome procrastination is to nibble away at an unwanted task; break it up into segments and tackle one segment at a time. If there is a task you would rather postpone, try waiting until tomorrow morning—and then do it first thing.

Joe Adams' Steps to Eliminate Time Wasters

Joe Adams, an expert on how companies can better use their time, often uses Friday morning to set the scene: "It is already the last day of the week and it seems like there's a week's worth of work still to be done." Sound familiar? He offers the following advice (see also Time Wasters for Every Day of the Month, at end of the chapter).

- **Step 1: Establish goals and priorities**—Make a list of long- and short-term priorities. Don't be afraid to change it, even hour-by-hour. Next, arrange the items on your list in the order of their importance. Divide them into related, specific tasks; start at the top of the list and tackle them, one at a time. An hourly appointment calendar or sheet is a good form to use.

- **Step 2: Delegate**—What can you delegate on your list? If you ask others to do a task, issue clear instructions, make sure they are understood, establish a deadline for the completion of the assignment, and plan to check up on its progress. Allow yourself a little leeway. If correction of work completed or clarity of instructions is required, you'll have a little time to do it—without panic.

- **Step 3: Pareto's rule/principle**—Eighty percent of your results are generated from 20 percent of your effort. You will maximize your time and get your best results if you concentrate on those 20 percent tasks that are critical to the completion of a project and delay or avoid those that contribute little to the success of the job.

- **Step 4: Leverage your peak energy time**—When are you at your best? Some of us have peak energy in the morning when we first start to work. This is the time to work on high-priority items; we can save the low-priority tasks for later, when our peak energy has ebbed.

- **Step 5: Group your day's activities**—Read all your mail at once. Make all your phone calls one after the other, taking notes on each on a continuous pad. Do all your figuring without interruption. Interrupting an activity that takes some concentration will demand mental "tooling up" to start it again. You'll improve your use of time and eliminate aggravation by doing each task in turn and completing it before jumping on to the next one.

- **Step 6: Interruptions**—They are inevitable. If there were none, chances are you would not be busy and in demand—and you wouldn't be of use to anyone. How do you handle the inevitable interruptions efficiently? If you have an assistant, ask that all extraneous matters be grouped so that you can take care of them at one time. Have incoming calls recorded so that you can respond to them all at once at your convenience. Schedule specific time periods for meetings, conferences, and visits.

- **Step 7: Paperwork**—Don't shuffle all those papers on your desk. Handle each one once, and do something with it after you've made a decision or dispose of it.

- **Step 8: The Tyranny of the Urgent**—Most people are more likely to respond to the urgent than to the important. The conflict between what is important and what is urgent can be summarized best by using the following four cells. What cell are you in? Two subtle points emerge from this principle:

1. There is no end to it. Tyranny of the Urgent is a battle we each will fight day after day for the rest of our lives.
2. Learn to say no nicely, if you can, but be nasty if you must. Learn to say no, so that you have the time for really important things in your life.

Knowing when to say no comes from understanding what is important to us. Planning allows us to do this. It makes important things equal in priority to urgent things and allows us to bring important things into the present. Once in the present, we can set priorities.

- **Step 9: Be realistic about how long a task will take**—Don't create your own pressure cooker. Leave yourself enough time to do a job. Like budgeting, time scheduling needs a little elasticity—and a little extra time between tasks—because tasks usually take more rather than less time. Always anticipate the unexpected.

- **Step 10: Efficiency versus effectiveness**—Doing a job right, versus doing the right job right, is an important concept to consider when eliminating time wasters. Apply the following formula to your next task:

$$E \text{ (Effectiveness)} = \frac{R \text{ (Results)}}{T \text{ (Time)}}$$

Complete the following Time Management Exercise. You will have to do many of the tasks yourself, but you can delegate some of them to someone else. See how many fall into the latter category—and how much time, effort, and frustration you can save yourself.

Tyranny of the Urgent
What cell am I in?

			Urgent	
			Yes	No
Yes		Yes	1	2
		IMPORTANT		
No		No	3	4

Time Management Exercise

Instructions: Place either an "M" (managerial) or "D" (delegate) next to each action statement below.

_____ 1. Calling on an account with one of your salespeople to show a customer that your company's management is interested in the account and to determine their business potential.

_____ 2. Making a sales presentation to a prospect in order to show one of your new salespeople how to do it.

_____ 3. Making a call to an office of a large key account in order to cement the relationship and promote future business.

_____ 4. Explaining how to solve a sales problem one of your people brought to you because he or she cannot solve it.

_____ 5. Filling out a performance appraisal with a member of your sales team.

_____ 6. Explaining to one of your salespeople why he or she is receiving some new accounts.

_____ 7. Interviewing a prospective sales representative referred to you by an employment agency.

_____ 8. Giving a telephone progress report of a current program to your manager.

_____ 9. Asking one of your salespeople what he or she thinks about a selling idea you have.

_____ 10. Stepping into a selling situation to save a deal while working with one of your salespeople.

_____ 11. Handling a large account's phone call yourself because your salesperson is unfamiliar with the customer.

_____ 12. Reviewing itineraries and sales call reports to determine progress toward reaching specific sales objectives.

_____ 13. Deciding whether to meet a competitive price beyond what the salesperson has access to.

_____ 14. Deciding whether to recommend adding another salesperson.

_____ 15. Correcting a mistake on one of your salesperson's orders before sending it in.

_____ 16. Asking your salesperson to establish objectives for the number of face-to-face sales calls to target an account or market.

_____ 17. Attending a business trade show with team members.

_____ 18. Transferring an account away from a sales rep because the rep wasn't paying enough attention to the customer.

_____ 19. Dictating a critical business proposal for one of your salespeople.

_____ 20. Closing on a phone order and arranging delivery for one of your salespeople's customers while he or she is on vacation.

Items 1, 3, 10, 11, 15, 17, 19 can be delegated; the others are management-type work.

The next exercise is a Time Log Analysis Guide. It is followed by a simple Task Time Analysis, which is followed by a Time Management Quiz. The results may surprise you.

Time Log Analysis Guide

Your effectiveness as a field sales management professional depends on the amount of time you spend developing your people. Thus, any effort to improve overall sales or service performance must focus on the vital hours spent with the salespeople who report to you. Use the following questions as a guide in making your time log analysis:

1. Based on what is expected of you:
   a. How does what you get paid for doing match your time usage log results?
   b. How does the log show that you are carrying out your boss's expectations?

2. For each function on your typical week's time usage form, ask:
   a. What would happen if this were not done at all?
   b. What would happen if this were left for later?
   c. Could someone else do this just as well if not better?

3. Did you set aside solid blocks of uninterrupted time for your most important tasks?   Yes ____ No____

4. Did you set weekly and daily goals during this week?   Yes ____ No____
   a. Were these goals challenging yet attainable?   Yes ____ No____
   b. Did these goals contribute to your long-range objectives?   Yes ____ No____
   c. Do you prioritize your goals?   Yes ____ No____

5. While keeping the log, what percentage of your time was spent face to face, elbow to elbow, making calls with your salespeople versus B and C activities? A's_____% B's_____% C's_____%

6. Look at the C's and ask:
   a. What C's occurred most frequently? _____
   _____

   b. What C's could I eliminate or reduce? _____
   _____

7. Look at your interruptions and ask:
   a. Who or what was my most frequent interrupter? _____
   _____

   b. What are the causes? _____
   _____

   c. How can I control, minimize, or eliminate the interrupter?
   _____

   d. Who do I most frequently interrupt? How often? Why?
   _____

8. Which phone calls, visits, trips, meetings, etc. could have been re-duced, eliminated, or done by someone else in the organ-ization?_____

9. How might I consolidate or eliminate routine items? _____
   _____

10. How did the findings on the weekly log compare to the primary goals (developing your people) on your "to do" list?

11. At the end of each logging day, ask:
    a. What time did I start working on my A-1 priority (face to face, developing people)?   Time_____
    b. Could I have started sooner?   Yes ___ No___
    c. Did anything distract me from completing it? Yes ___ No___
       What? _____
       Why? _____
    d. Could I have avoided the distraction?   Yes ___ No___
    e. Did I recover immediately and return to   Yes ___ No___
       task?
    f. What might I have done differently this week? _____
    _____

12. What percentage of time did you spend in meetings? _____%
    a. What did you accomplish at meetings? _____

    _____

    b. Was this meeting necessary?   Yes ___ No___
    c. Did the meeting have an agenda?   Yes ___ No___
    d. Was the agenda adhered to?   Yes ___ No___
    e. Did the meeting start on time?   Yes ___ No___
    f. Did the meeting end on time?   Yes ___ No___

Note: Peter Drucker suggests sending a memo to cut down on time wasted in meetings: I have invited (names) to meet with me (date/time/place) to discuss (subject). Please come if you think that you need the information or want to take part in the discussion. But you will, in any event, receive right away a full summary of the discussion and a copy of any decisions reached, together with a request for your comments.

13. How much of the week was free or uncommitted?   Time _____

14. What was the longest period of completely uninterrupted time?

    _____

    a. What part of the week was most productive? _____

    _____

    Why? _____

    b. What was least productive? _____

    _____

    Why? _____

    c. Is this a normal pattern?   Yes ___ No___
    d. Do you plan around your high/low energy   Yes ___ No___
       cycles?
    e. How could you make other periods of the week just as productive?

    _____

    _____

Note: It is suggested that you put extra time logs similar to the one you have completed in your six-month tickler file. Then, force yourself to once again record and analyze your time. We are all creatures of habit, and unless we monitor our own progress, we tend to fall back into old and less effective practices. The time log allows us to reward ourselves when we do find solid improvement in our time management and to identify behavior patterns that may need further modification.

Task Time Analysis

Sales Management Functional Area	% Time Spent	% Importance
1. _____	_____	_____
2. _____	_____	_____
3. _____	_____	_____
4. _____	_____	_____
5. _____	_____	_____
6. _____	_____	_____
7. _____	_____	_____
8. _____	_____	_____
9. _____	_____	_____
10. _____	_____	_____

What am I spending too much time on? _____
_____

What am I spending too little time on? _____
_____

What can I delegate? _____
_____

Time Management Quiz

	True	False
1. Most managers are overworked due to the nature of the job.	____	____
2. Each manager's job is unique and not subject to repetitive time patterns.	____	____
3. No manager ever has enough time.	____	____
4. Decisions made at a higher level are usually better decisions.	____	____

5. Delay will enable you to improve the quality of your decisions. ____ ____

6. Most managers probably can find many ways to save time. ____ ____

7. Managing your time better is essentially a matter of reducing the time spent on various activities. ____ ____

8. Managers deal with people, and because all people are important, you cannot establish priorities. ____ ____

9. Delegating probably will free up a great deal of time and relieve you of some responsibility. ____ ____

10. Finding blocks of time is impossible, especially in small offices. ____ ____

11. Most managers probably can solve time problems by working harder. ____ ____

12. Managers who concentrate on working efficiently are most effective. ____ ____

13. If you want it done right, you'd better do it yourself. ____ ____

14. Most ordinary day-to-day activities do not need to be planned. ____ ____

15. Working on priorities is not possible. ____ ____

16. Finding the problem is easy; finding the solution is difficult. ____ ____

17. A good way to reduce wasted time is to look for shortcuts in managerial functions. ____ ____

18. Most managers can easily identify their biggest time wasters. ____ ____

19. If you really managed your time well, you would be a robot. ____ ____

20. Busy and active managers who work the hardest get the best results. ____ ____

21. If you really try to control time, you'll miss out on unexpected opportunities. ____ ____

22. Time management does not allow for spontaneous   ____ ____
    behavior; it is dull and mechanical.

23. Writing objectives is a waste.   ____ ____

24. The most important results are produced with the   ____ ____
    greatest input of time.

25. My astrological sign is inconsistent with being   ____ ____
    organized.

The answers to the foregoing quiz all are false. Chances are, you aren't surprised!

Focus and Finish

Concentrate on the important task first, and then complete it before going on to the next project. It helps to curtail confusion and wasting time.

Time Wasters for Every Day of the Month

1 Drop-in visitors	2 Unscheduled meetings	3 Putting out minor fires	4 Lack of objectives	5 Lack of deadlines	6 Lack of priorities	7 Desk clutter
8 Personal disorgan-ization	9 Vague delegation	10 Doing a lot of dull tasks yourself	11 Trying to do too much	12 Unrealistic time estimates	13 Ineffectual communi-cations	14 Insufficiently trained assistant
15 Procrast-ination	16 Day-dreaming	17 Indecision	18 Inability to say no	19 Leaving small jobs for tomorrow	20 Jumping from one task to another	21 Getting involved in too much detail
22 Social-izing to no purpose	23 Haste that makes waste	24 Diverting personal projects	25 Extrane-ous reading matter, junk mail	26 Inefficient or non-working equipment	27 Periods of fatigue & boredom	28 Writing too many memos & reports
29 Failure to listen to others	30 Tendency to blame others					

CHAPTER 11

Performance Management

Now that you have selected and oriented your new applicants, the next task is to develop their sales performance. According to sales management ace Jack Falvey, "Salespeople's biggest challenge is not to learn their business, but their customer's business." According to Falvey, sales performance should consist of:

- 80 percent field training
- 15 percent product or service training
- 5 percent developing selling skills

Yet each facet in developing sales performance is vital. Each is a spoke in the wheel, and if any one is missing, it could cause the wheel to collapse and ruin the sale.

Sales performance is based as much on technical know-how and personal know-how as it is on practical psychology. Whereas specific skills can be learned in an hour's training session, only long periods of actual exposure in the field will motivate salespeople to master their profession.

First of all, remember that you are the *sales manager*. Your job is to get the task done through your sales reps, not to do it yourself. There is no need to prove that you can sell. If you had not already proven that, you would probably not be in the position of managing others.

If selling ability were the only criterion for hiring you, chances are that someone who had an even more brilliant sales record would have been selected. As a manager, you may occasionally be tempted to show off. After all, you have been, and still are, a darn good salesperson.

However, that's no longer your job. Resist the temptation to show off. Your ability to sell was not the prime reason for your promotion.

As sales manager, your management task is to visit the troops in the field. This is usually a one-on-one event. Tell your sales rep that you are merely there to see and learn. Above all, resist any temptation to "carry the bag."

Before you make a joint sales or service call with your field rep, discuss each customer or prospect's personality, history, and needs. It is vital that you hold this discussion before the sales call. By doing so, you can comfortably resist the temptation to jump into the discussion and either show your superiority or kill any future motivation for the sales rep who is left holding the bag.

Do not expect perfection from sales reps. They can fail and have every right to do so. You hope they won't, but they are human. A rep might not be feeling well, may have had little sleep because of a sick child, may have had a fight with his or her spouse, and so on. Allow for a little leeway and even compassion in your management style.

Developing trust is one of the hallmarks of performance management. Tell your reps that you are there to get to know them, to learn firsthand about their problems, to reiterate your goals, to pick up new ideas—and to show the customer that your company cares.

Listening and observing can be even more important to a salesperson's progress and sales success than actively participating. "How can I help you?" can be a better incentive than showing off your superiority.

When you become a sales manager, you will most likely have replaced another one. Your predecessor might have had different philosophies and different methods—and certainly a different personality. Your predecessor's opinions will likely be raised, and you need to be ready to accept them or adjust them if they differ from yours. Try not to reject them outright, but temper them with logic and reason if yours are different.

Personality differences are bound to occur. You will likely have to evaluate reps who are older than you, more experienced, and with a variety of personality types. Your own wisdom and judgment will be called upon to smooth over any lack of dovetailing opinions, beliefs, and methods. Only logic and reason will make another, perhaps older and more experienced individual, accept your management style. A more abrasive method could lead to a parting of the ways—but make sure the salesperson isn't the president's brother-in-law. As they say in the military, "Never burn your bridges behind you; you might have to retreat over them."

Ultimately, you will be the one to judge the sales rep's performance. There is only one criterion upon which you should rely: results. The key is that everyone is different. Style, personality, looks, and interests are pieces of the whole person, but in the final analysis, you must be looking for results.

Why Don't People Perform?

This question usually comes up when the results we are looking for aren't there. It is a simple question, and it has simple answers:

- **They don't know what is expected of them**—We haven't provided them with performance standards to do the job. Sometimes, they get a job description, but it does not spell out the performance standards for the job.
- **They don't know how to perform**—We haven't provided the training for those job skills in which they are weak.
- **They don't want to**—We haven't created an environment that motivates them to do the job.
- **We get in their way**—In many instances, we just haven't gotten out of their way to let them perform.

Can you judge a job without standards? If there are no standards, how do you know if a rep is doing a good job or a bad job? You don't. You are guessing. The benefit of establishing performance standards is that they tell sales reps what is expected of them. Therefore, a standard is a finite expression of a performance expectation. Good standards are like effective goals, they must be Specific, Measurable, Attainable, Realistic. and Time-bound.

Securing an Understanding of the Job

There is a three-part process for securing an understanding of a job. This is a practical way to secure an understanding of the "what" of a job, as well as helping to decide when a job is well-done.

- **Major tasks**—Start by defining the major responsibilities for which your sales reps are accountable (i.e., sales volume, territory coverage, reports and records, expenses, etc.).
- **Indicators of performance**—Develop data agreed upon by you and your sales reps to determine how well they are accomplishing their responsibilities. Evidence of results should answer the following question for your sales reps: "What do I want my boss to take into account when he or she reviews my performance?" The evidence should also answer the manager's question: "What am I going to take into account in determining when a job has been done well?"
- **Standards of performance**—Define the end result which, if secured, will represent reasonable or outstanding performance.

An example of a Performance Standards Worksheet follows. Also included is the Sales Manager Standards of Performance (Generic) which lists 10 standards and the chapters within which the reader can find the answer to the questions: What is reasonable performance? and what is outstanding performance?

Sales Manager Standards of Performance (Generic)

The Sales Manager:

Standard of Performance	Book Chapter
1. Recruits, selects and hires sales personnel	5
2. Provides performance improvement training to a sales depaartment employees	6
3. Uses a prospecting and follow up system for recruiting new salespeople	5
4. Operates and maintains a selling system used by of his or her all sales personnel	10
5. Coaches, supervises, and direct sales personnel according to established sales objectives	3, 4
6. Manages a well-maintained selling environment	3
7. Prepares and monitors sales and profit budges and forecasts	4
8. Assist in developing and executing advertising and promotion plans	15
9. Establishes and maintains effective working relationships with other managers	15
10. Maintains a professional presence at all times	3, 4

Example of a Sales Person's Performance Standards Worksheet

Responsibility	Indicators of Performance	Standard of Performance
		What is reasonable perf?/ What is outstanding perf?
Sales Volume	1. # of widgets sold/day/week/qtr. 2. # of budgeted cases (quota) 3. Cases this year vs. last year 4. New accounts opened/month 5. Dollar volume sold/shipped 6. Gained/lost distribution 7. Key account development	
Territory Coverage	1. Calls made per day/week 2. Decision makers seen per day/week 3. Presentations made per day/week 4. Sales closed per day/week 5. First time calls made per day/week 6. Prospects closed per week 7. Coverage of assigned calls 8. Routings and call-backs	
Reports and Records	1. Timeliness & Completeness 2. Accuracy 3. Competitive Activity (#) 4. Up-to-dateness of computer files 5. Weekly itinerary transmitted	
Expense Control	1. Company car expense 2. Entertainment $'s 3. Samples $'s 4. Supplies 5. Telephone 6. Total expense	

Advertising & Promotion
Protection of Company Property
Personal Development
Relationships

Setting Performance Standards: Personal Example

To get a point across to trainees, try using a subject dear to everyone's heart: taking a vacation. Dramatize it explaining three required steps that should lead to happy results:

- Establish what it takes or what is needed to go on vacation.
- Determine the steps that need to be taken or benchmarks.
- Consider the results or standards that you want to achieve.

Here is a sample checklist:

Tasks
- Determine the destination
- Set dates (When and for how long can you go?)
- Budget (How much do you have to spend?)
- Transportation (By what means will you be traveling?)
- Reservations (Have a travel agent make them or call directly?)
- Participants (Who goes on the trip? If kids are left at home, what arrangements need to be made?)
- Research (Gather information from literature, friends, family, co-workers, tourist bureaus, etc.)
- Expected pleasures (What do you expect in the way of recreation, sightseeing, eating, shopping, etc?)

Indicators
- Evaluate various optional destinations
- Survey personal likes and dislikes of participants
- Check on the weather at that time of year and plan appropriate wardrobe
- Transportation (check transportation and schedules)
- Gather and study available literature and information
- Payments (assure availability of funds and reserves)
- Schedule (make sure travel plans fit into business or job time frame)
- Confirmations (assure that plans are firm)
- Clear mind (make sure all job- or business-related problems are assigned or taken care of)

Standards
- Review (Did you have a good time and accomplish what you anticipated?)

- Plans (Did your planning, timing, and budget work out as anticipated? If not, what changes could you make the next time?)
- Review (If all was satisfactory, will you use these performance
  standards again?)

How to Increase Your Sales Performance 20 Percent

Define the key habits of your (or any) best salesperson and then
teach them to an average performer. His or her output will go
up 20 percent.

—Gerald O'Shea
Performance Management, Inc., Scarsdale, New York

Appraisal Techniques

Conducting performance evaluations is one of the primary responsibilities of a district or branch manager or, for that matter, any manager. One
of the important tasks is to conduct an objective and accurate evaluation
of the men and women you manage. It would be impossible to offer
effective training without pinpointing those areas that require additional
help. Only relevant evaluation will enable you to do that.

Suppose you see the need for training in some specific areas, but one
of your salespeople does not. Her perception of her need might differ 180
degrees from yours. If you do not explain this need thoroughly and
convince her of its importance, she might resent your efforts. Even worse,
she will not absorb the message, despite your sincerest efforts.

The following pointers, based on my many years of experience in
training managers on techniques of conducting evaluations, will help you
maximize the effectiveness of your efforts.

1. The Salesperson Evaluation Form (see next page) is an opening or
   invitation to salespeople to evaluate themselves and arrive at some
   of their own conclusions. Set a time limit for self-evaluations,
   probably no more than one week. Let your salespeople know that
   you, too, will make the identical evaluation and that you will then
   get together, compare notes, discuss differences, and develop an
   action for improvements that might be needed.

2. Complete the form for each of your salespeople. Take your time and
   be as objective and honest as possible. The form should include a

category for "needs help," which either of you can check, for each area rated.

3. Within a week following receipt of the evaluation sheet, you and the salesperson must get together for a review. Pick a place where you will not be interrupted for as long you think it will take to complete your session. Compare differences, if any. Then listen carefully and politely to your salesperson's reasons for the higher ratings first and then the lower ratings. Explain your higher rating and then your lower ratings, but do not make any changes in your evaluation at this time.

4. Needed improvements must be specific and performed within a specific time frame. Tell your salesperson exactly how such improvements can be made and help him or her remember and practice them. Offer your continued help, and be firm about reviewing the problem within a week or two. Saying "I am here to help you make more money" might be one way to underscore the need for improvement.

5. Establish an improvement plan for all items below acceptable levels.

6. Be careful not to fall into the trap of "whitewashing" the evaluation. It is easy to reduce your work load and to make your team look good. Be assured that this is a trap, because if the performance evaluation shows up serious weaknesses and they remain uncorrected, they will surely show up at a later time in your sales or performance figures. Sweeping problems under the rug will not get rid of the dirt.

Salesperson Evaluation Form

Salesperson: Mary Smith   **Evaluation conducted by SELF** _____

                                                                    MGR _X_

Category	Excellent									Poor	Needs Help
Telephone sales presentation	10	9	8	7	6	5	4	3	2	1	_____
Timely submission of reports	10	9	8	7	6	5	4	3	2	1	_____
Accuracy of reports	10	9	8	7	6	5	4	3	2	1	_____
Time & territory management	10	9	8	7	6	5	4	3	2	1	_____
Maintains accurate records	10	9	8	7	6	5	4	3	2	1	_____

Records well-organized	10	9	8	7	6	5	4	3	2	1	____
Pre-call planning	10	9	8	7	6	5	4	3	2	1	____
SMART sales call objectives	10	9	8	7	6	5	4	3	2	1	____
Knowledge of competition	10	9	8	7	6	5	4	3	2	1	____
Knowledge of products/service	10	9	8	7	6	5	4	3	2	1	____
Face-to-face presentations	10	9	8	7	6	5	4	3	2	1	____
Strong opening statement	10	9	8	7	6	5	4	3	2	1	____
Presents customer benefits	10	9	8	7	6	5	4	3	2	1	____
Handling objections	10	9	8	7	6	5	4	3	2	1	____
Closing skills	10	9	8	7	6	5	4	3	2	1	____
Questioning skills	10	9	8	7	6	5	4	3	2	1	____
Listening skills	10	9	8	7	6	5	4	3	2	1	____
Reliability	10	9	8	7	6	5	4	3	2	1	____
Establishes priorities	10	9	8	7	6	5	4	3	2	1	____
Post-call analysis	10	9	8	7	6	5	4	3	2	1	____
Self-development activities	10	9	8	7	6	5	4	3	2	1	____

Improvement and training needed: _____

_____

Action plan: _____

_____

What: _____

By when: _____

Comments: _____

5 Steps to Effective Performance Management

The performance management process follows a well-defined and proven path. Many years of experience of sales training professionals from the Professional Society of Sales and Marketing Training (SMT) have demonstrated the following to be highly effective:

- Step 1: Set objectives
- Step 2: Action planning
- Step 3: GAP (general action plan) analysis
- Step 4: Formal evaluation
- Step 5: Renewing the process

Let's dissect and review each of the five steps.

Step 1: Set objectives—This is the beginning of the performance management process. It establishes individual objectives for:

- Annual sales
- Business growth
- Professional growth

These three objectives all work together to improve your company's sales. Establishing both organizational and individual objectives is the crucial step in the performance management process. In order for these objectives to be effective and of benefit to both the individual and the company, they must be formed together at the same time. If the results are good for the company, they are also good for the individual—and vice versa. Working together for each other's benefit is called symbiosis. Like any contact or agreement, it is good only if both parties agree to it and benefit from it.

Let's look at an example. A company decides that in order to remain viable and profitable, sales dollar volume must grow by 18 to 22 percent. The individual objectives of sales representatives must, of course, reflect this company goal. How can this be accomplished? Individual sales managers might be directed to increase the number and frequency of calls—especially on specific major accounts whose volume purchases can help reach the objective more quickly.

The key to establishing objectives is to channel individual and organization energy toward a common goal. An effective way to reach these objectives is the SMART way.

Step 2: Action planning—This puts the "arms and legs" on the performance objectives. Experienced managers can help their sales teams select the most effective ways to reach their individual performance objectives. Together they can create standards of performance that allow their sales teams to measure their progress at various key points during the year. At the end of this chapter (p. 163), you'll find an example of a weekly performance standards chart for:

- Making sales calls
- Seeing decision makers
- Making presentations
- Closing sales

- Making first-time calls
- Closing prospects

Such a general action plan (GAP) allows you to analyze what went right and what went wrong. It makes sales management easier and more productive. It answers your sales staff's most common request: "Help me, don't tell me."

Step 3: GAP analysis—Observing, coaching, and training again involve the SMART method. The sales manager and his or her sales team become partners in establishing goals that are:

Specific as opposed to general and ill-defined
Measurable in terms of results desired, instead of just grandstanding
Attainable in the minds of both the company executives in the
    office and the men and women in the field
Realistic in the face of internal and external economic conditions
Time-bound so that everyone understands the demands of the
    clock and the calendar (the fifth dimension)

To achieve these mutually agreed-upon goals, the sales manager must:

1. Evaluate individual strengths and weaknesses
2. Develop training and on-the-job strategies to promote the strengths and correct observed weaknesses
3. Plan for frequent feedback

New sales team members in particular require close, careful observation, which is critical so that performance problems can be solved early. You can only effect solutions if you know the problems. The amount of observation an individual receives depends on the personality, experience, and ambition of the individual. Such observation is the basis for training and coaching, as well as fair performance measurements. Some people will require a great deal of effort; for others, occasional meetings may suffice. Your own time is valuable, so hiring and retaining the right team member is important to the company—as well as to you.

This step requires a great deal of flexibility and responsiveness from all team members. During this century's final decade, we know that nontraditional demands often become traditional areas. It is incumbent on each of us, in sales management was well as on the sales team, to be flexible, to adapt, and to grow as the demands of the job change. Sales managers must be equally responsive to staff needs for support, coaching, and training. We cannot afford to be inflexible any longer. Dinosaurs were.

Step 4: Formal evaluation—This requires periodic formal evaluation. Timing is of the essence. Interviews need to be scheduled frequently enough to give you an objective handle on effective performance, but not so often that they will overburden you and your salespeople with paperwork. Establishing standards for such interviews, with equal time and care spent on each case, will give all salespeople essentially the same consideration. Your own mature, experienced judgment will be the best guide.

Remember that the purpose of a formal performance appraisal interview is not to criticize or flatter but to objectively and candidly assess what your salesperson has accomplished.

Putting Step 4 to work can best be achieved by keeping these points in mind:

1. How will this performance review differ from any of the coaching sessions?
2. Performance reviews should give equal time and care to each person participating in them.
3. Review leads naturally to setting next year's objectives, including professional development and skills needed to make next year a great one for everyone.
4. Performance reviews can be an additional benefit—as a powerful motivator.

Step 5: Renewing the process—After the formal evaluation, it is time to renew the entire process by reviewing and, as is usually the case, revisiting individual objectives.

Once new objectives have been set and agreed upon by both management and the sales staff, both can develop action plans for reaching those objectives (remember the SMART approach). The new objectives should include training, retraining, and coaching.

The result of such performance reviews should be, as noted in item 4 above, additional motivation for excellence. Sales managers and trainers should therefore establish their own four goals:

- To reward excellence
- To remedy weakness
- To provide direction
- To generate enthusiasm

J.W. Marriott, Jr., chairman of the Marriott Corporation, put it correctly:

> Motivate them, train them, care about them, and make winners out of them. If we treat our employees correctly, they'll treat the customers right. And if customers are treated right, they'll come back.

And that, after all, is what our quality efforts are about.

Conducting a Sales Performance Audit

The increasing complexity of today's selling climate, abetted by fiercer competition, both domestic and foreign, makes it mandatory that we avail ourselves of all tools at our disposal. One of them is the sales performance audit (SPA), which allows us to analyze our organization, our environment, and the individual salespeople.

The goals of the SPA are twofold:

1. It gives your company a comprehensive overview of its sales organization and the performance problems it might be experiencing.
2. SPA identifies, in cost-versus-benefit terms, the steps management can take to increase sales.

The first step in the SPA is the organizational overview. It summarizes the:

- Goals and structure of the existing sales organization
- Resources and support services your staff needs
- Environment in which the staff operates
- Skills and information required
- Appropriate motivation and compensation
- Management help required for an effective sales effort

The second in the SPA step includes recognition that a feedback system is needed. It is usually more economical than putting on time- and money-intensive workshops. The questions an effective feedback system answers are:

- Is the salesperson's concept of sales goals and responsibility clear?
- Is the salesperson informed about correct and incorrect performance?
- What awards—and punishment—does the salesperson receive for correct or incorrect sales performance?

As a sales manager, you should be cognizant of top management's concerns. You will have no trouble having their answers if you know what is expected. Management or corporate concerns fall generally into five categories:

- Does the sales manager have a clear understanding of what sales-people should be doing?
- Has the sales manager established clear goals and objectives that the average salesperson can understand and achieve?
- Does the sales manager structure assignments appropriately for the average rep?
- Does the sales manager coach (train) salespeople to correct deficiencies?
- When support is needed, is appropriate staff available to assist salespeople?

The SPA is presented below as a convenient chart. Determine which of the functions indicated would be applicable to your business. Mark recommended actions, preferably in order of importance or feasibility.

Organization Analysis	Environmental Analysis	Individual Salespeople Analysis
__ Product positioning	__ Environmental	__ Salespeople's skills
__ Market segments	constraints	__ Salespeople's
__ Sales goals	__ Support staff	knowledge
__ Plans & assignments	availability	__ Salespeople's
__ Targeted accounts	__ Resources	attitude
__ Key account targets	__ Sales aids	
__ Territory assignments	__ System access	
__ Customer database	__ Feedback consequences	
system	__ Incentives	

Identifying the Sales Manager's Job

Management consultants Sandra J. and Roger J. Plachy of Winston- Salem, North Carolina, have dissected the essential job of the sales manager. The result of their work is a useful compilation or test to employ in performance management—or in evaluating yourself.

A sales manager, whose principal jobs are to implement national sales plans and supervise regional sales managers or salespersons, can judge himself or herself by how well the following are performed:

1. **Determines annual unit and gross profit plans** by implementing marketing strategies and analyzing trends and results of previous periods. Example:
   - Previous period sales results = $24 million
   - Average unit selling price for previous period = $8
   - Annual increase that can realistically be achieved = 20 percent
   - Annual unit plan for $30 million = 3,750,000 units
   - Gross profit = $19,230,000 or 35.9 percent

   Sales managers in large and small companies alike must learn how to sell budgets. They are actually major "account" sales that must be made each year (and resold every quarter) according to Jack Falvey's regular article in the November 1991 issue of *Sales & Marketing Management* magazine.

2. **Establishes sales objectives** by forecasting and developing annual sales quotas for regions and territories and by projecting expected sales volume and profit for existing and new products. (Note that a sales quota is higher than an objective, which is a psychological factor in helping achieve the objective.) For example, using the top-down and bottom-up approach in forecasting regional sales, managers would obtain input from each territory salesperson on sales quotas. If there are five regions and all are equal in volume, then each would look like this:
   - Annual sales quota per region = $5.5 million
   - Existing product sales = $4.9 million
   - New product sales = $0.6 million
   - Number of territories = 5
   - Annual sales quota per territory = $1.1 million

3. **Implements national sales programs** by developing field sales action plans.

4. **Maintains sales volume, product mix, and selling price** by keeping current with supply and demand, changing trends, and economic indicators, as well as competitors.

5. **Establishes and adjusts selling prices** by monitoring costs, competition, and supply and demand.

6. **Completes national sales operational requirements** by scheduling and assigning employees and following up on work results.

7. **Maintains national sales staff** by recruiting, selecting, orienting, and training employees. For example, in order to develop future sales managers, it is going to take 12 to 24 months to launch them successfully in their careers as new field sales managers.

8. **Maintains national sales staff results** by counseling and disciplining employees and planning, monitoring, and appraising job results.

9. **Maintains professional and technical knowledge** by attending educational workshops (especially negotiating courses to help with each year's "battle of the budget" meetings), reviewing professional publications, establishing personal networks, and participating in professional societies (i.e., Sales and Marketing Executives, the Professional Society of Sales and Marketing Training, etc.).

10. **Contributes to team efforts** by accomplishing related results as needed.

You might want to jot down the amount of time you spend on each of the ten functions and analyze the time spent in relation to the importance of the function. This time study will be even more important when measuring the job performance of others.

To Measure Performance Realistically, Hold Salespeople Responsible Weekly

If you set goals for the long haul or are vague in the goals you want to reach, chances are you are going to miss your target figures by a mile. Salespeople don't understand a goal or performance figures that are vague and non-specific. If you want to assure results, you have to create daily goals. State very directly how many calls, presentations, or demonstrations you want made. Clarify that these calls and presentations must be made to decision makers. You will see positive results almost immediately.

Ask for suggestions. You will be surprised by how many ideas the salespeople in the field have, ideas developed from field experience with which they are comfortable.

Don't take for granted that your salespeople know their goals or responsibilities. Ask them to write them down, individually. You might be surprised—shocked, perhaps—by what these men and women do not know. Too many salespeople are not actively pursuing leads and sales; too many wait for leads or calls to come in by themselves. The reality is that while these passive salespeople twiddle their thumbs, competitors are out there making the calls.

All these facts need to be communicated to the sales team at least once a week; the company's goals or mission statement has to be clarified. Management has to lead by example, and you have to check in frequently to make sure the sales team understands these goals.

Performance Evaluation

To be used by:
- Salespeople to monitor their own progress after each sales call or at least weekly
- Sales managers when coaching a sales call
- Sales trainers to rate individual salespeople or to audit a field office or branch
- Companies that want to conduct an annual (or more frequent) sales staff audit

For the purpose of:
- Evaluating your sales team's strengths
- Identifying areas that could use improvement
- Monitoring ongoing sales training efforts
- Reminding your salespeople that you truly care about their performance and want to help them

Sales Performance Evaluation

Salesperson: _____

Observer: _____

Customer/Client: _____

Date: _____   Time: _____

Note: Evaluation should be done in private and with great deliberation. Make notes in areas for further coaching or learning needs. Review with salesperson observed.

Rating scale: 0 = did not observe   3 = satisfactory
                1 = unsatisfactory   4 = above average
                2 = needs improvement   5 = superior

Sales Call Preparation

Account information review	0 1 2 3 4 5
Determination of competitiveness	0 1 2 3 4 5
Set a SMART sales call objective	0 1 2 3 4 5

Client Contact

Relating to the receptionist	0 1 2 3 4 5
Reach the decision maker	0 1 2 3 4 5
Rapport with customer/client	0 1 2 3 4 5
Purpose of call and agenda discussed	0 1 2 3 4 5
Overcome concerns	0 1 2 3 4 5

Fact Finding

Quality of high gain questions	0 1 2 3 4 5
Uncovering specific customer needs	0 1 2 3 4 5
Smooth flow of discussion	0 1 2 3 4 5
Identifying major customer concerns	0 1 2 3 4 5
Being a good listener	0 1 2 3 4 5
Determining customer satisfaction	0 1 2 3 4 5
Establish a competitive position	0 1 2 3 4 5

Presentation

Presenting customer's needs/wants	0 1 2 3 4 5
Clarifying customer's benefits/results	0 1 2 3 4 5
Justifying costs	0 1 2 3 4 5
Answering customer's concerns	0 1 2 3 4 5
Quality of written/verbal communication	0 1 2 3 4 5
Thoroughness of product knowledge	0 1 2 3 4 5

Resistance

Anticipating customer's concerns	0	1	2	3	4	5
Addressing customer's fears	0	1	2	3	4	5
Transforming fears into assets	0	1	2	3	4	5
Overcoming objections	0	1	2	3	4	5

Closing

Recognizing/responding to buying signals	0	1	2	3	4	5
Asking for the order	0	1	2	3	4	5
Reemphasizing the close	0	1	2	3	4	5
Using silence when advantageous	0	1	2	3	4	5
Obtaining a clear, lasting commitment	0	1	2	3	4	5

Follow-Up

Thank customer for presentation time	0	1	2	3	4	5
Explaining next step in transaction	0	1	2	3	4	5
Discuss possible referrals	0	1	2	3	4	5
Complete all pertinent documentation	0	1	2	3	4	5
Writing post-meeting thank-you note	0	1	2	3	4	5
Overall Rating	0	1	2	3	4	5

Comments regarding further coaching needs: _____
_____

Sales Management Performance Feedback

Everybody needs feedback, including company presidents and sales managers. One of the best sources for this feedback is your sales staff.

Feedback can be obtained from subordinates and peers as well as from superiors and customers; it can even come from competitors' representatives. Some call this kind of feedback intelligence networking.

Let's look at an example. Sales manager Ed Jackson is scheduled to attend a workshop on performance management. There are 25 areas about which information, objective and subjective, will be sought. Put yourself in Ed's shoes and answer each of the following statements according to the instructions and evaluation key shown below.

Performance Counseling Questionnaire

Name of Manager: _____Ed Jackson_____

Instructions: Your manager, Ed Jackson, will soon be attending a workshop on performance management. As part of Ed's development, your thoughts about his current practices will benefit everyone involved. You will be one of up to four of his subordinates who will be completing this questionnaire. Your individual responses will not be identified because all responses will be grouped together.

Answer Part 1. Then, answer Part 2 only if you have at some time had a performance appraisal discussion with this manager (regardless of the length of the discussion). Circle the response that describes your reaction to each statement. (SA = strongly agree, A = agree, N = neither agree nor disagree, D = disagree, SD = strongly disagree.)

Return the questionnaire in the envelope provided. Make sure that *your manager's name* appears in the space provided at the top of this page.

Part 1

1. My manager is thorough in providing feedback on good performance as well as performance that needs improvement.   SA   A   N   D   SD

2. There are precise sales goals or objectives for my territory, so I know what has to be accomplished.   SA   A   N   D   SD

3. I have an opportunity to participate in setting goals and objectives for my area of responsibility.   SA   A   N   D   SD

4. I am aware of the purpose or mission of my area and how it contributes to my manager's mission.   SA   A   N   D   SD

5. My manager is clear about what he/she expects of me.   SA   A   N   D   SD

6. I have a reasonably up-to-date job description, which outlines my present role and general responsibilities.   SA   A   N   D   SD

7. My manager is willing to help me figure out what I have to do to improve my performance if needed.   SA   A   N   D   SD

8. He/she is interested in my career development and progress.   SA A N D SD

9. My manager provides me with the information I need to be effective.   SA A N D SD

10. My manager is flexible and realistic in adjusting his/her performance expectations if the circumstances warrant.   SA A N D SD

11. I am held accountable for the results my area achieves or fails to achieve.   SA A N D SD

12. If I fail to meet an expectation of my manager, I am confident he/she would help me learn from my mistakes.   SA A N D SD

13. My manager sometimes solicits my feedback on how I think he/she can improve as a manager.   SA A N D SD

14. I believe I can talk openly and honestly with my manager.   SA A N D SD

15. I have a clear picture of where I stand and what my future can be with the company.   SA A N D SD

Part 2 (if you have had an appraisal)

16. The performance appraisal(s) I have received has (have) been frequent enough to let me know how I am doing.   SA A N D SD

17. My manager allowed enough time for a thorough discussion of my performance.   SA A N D SD

18. He/she was fair and reasonable in assessing both my strengths and the areas needing further improvement.   SA A N D SD

19. When we began the performance discussion, I was clear about the purpose of the conversation.   SA A N D SD

20. My manager solicited my views on how well I was performing.   SA A N D SD

21. He/she is an effective listener.   SA A N D SD

22. If I provided constructive criticism to my   SA   A   N   D   SD
    manager about his/her performance or the
    company, he/she would not likely become
    defensive.

23. The performance appraisal discussion(s), while   SA   A   N   D   SD
    not always what I like to hear, help me
    improve and grow.

24. He/she helped me formulate goals beneficial   SA   A   N   D   SD
    to my career development and progress.

25. Overall, my manager does an effective job in   SA   A   N   D   SD
    managing my performance.

The Performance Skills of Sales Managers

Like all managers, sales managers divide their time among five classic
functions:

- **Planning**—Determining what work must be done
- **Organizing**—Dividing planned work into manageable units
- **Staffing**—Interviewing and hiring people to ensure that company
  plans can be carried out and goals achieved
- **Leading**—Training and supervising the staff within the company
  so that plans can be carried out and goals achieved
- **Controlling**—Assuring that company objectives are accomplished
  by:
  a. Establishing performance standards
  b. Monitoring and measuring these standards
  c. Taking corrective action, the means to an end

> If you use the right training philosophy,
> you won't be left out!

> - What I hear, I forget,
> - What I see, I remember,
> - What I do, I understand.

Performance Standards Scorecard

Week of:_____   Week # (out of 52):_____   Salesperson/Sales #_____

Daily Standards

Day/Date	Calls Made	Decision Makers Seen	Presentations Made	Sales Closed	First-Time Calls Made	Prospects Closed	Problem Areas
	Time management	Pre-approach and getting in the door		Making the presentation Closing the sale Objections Product knowledge	Prospecting Making the presentation Handling objections		

CHAPTER 12

Managing Sales Meetings

Most people would agree that meetings are a necessary evil. Some even see them as a sign that the person calling them is insecure. Meetings are also the subject of puns. Will Rogers said, "Outside of traffic, there is nothing that sets this country back as much as committees." Milton Berle added, "Committee—a group of men who keep minutes and waste hours." Even the staid Arthur Goldberg, former associate justice of the Supreme Court, said, "If Columbus had an advisory committee, he would probably still be at the dock."

Still, there is a positive side to meetings. The keys are in planning, goal setting, and getting full participation. Sales meetings are a good setting in which to exchange information and engage in training. Meetings can also be held to brainstorm and learn, two more valuable reasons. A meeting can serve as a public forum at which important company statements are made to all who have a stake in what happens to the company.

Meetings are the quickest and easiest way to gain commitment to yourself and your company's programs. The Professional Society for Sales and Marketing Training says, "Getting your salespeople to participate actively in meetings is more than just a good idea. *Today,* it's absolutely necessary for success!"

Over a period of more than 30 years, I was involved in every conceivable type of sales meeting at one of America's major corporations—training meetings, resort and office meetings, and regional and national half-day and day-long meetings. Distilling this experience, my recommendations for a successful meeting include the following ten suggestions:

1. Your meeting must have a theme and an objective.

2. Just like a sales letter, your meeting must have a strong opening and a memorable closing. This usually requires work and planning.

3. You need to maintain control over your audience. Because they will hardly be children, this has to be done through the importance of your message and through techniques to keep the meeting flowing along with its purpose.

4. Set a time and create an agenda, and stick to both. Controlling time is important, especially if you are going to have more meetings in the future.

5. If the audience is your own staff, you can use some tactics to increase attention and encourage punctuality. You can, for example, tack a few dollar bills to the bottom of the chairs and call attention to them at the beginning of the meeting, or charge all latecomers a dollar, which will then be pooled and used in a way that benefits the group.

6. Have a light catered lunch. This will allow the group to network with each other and will cut down on the length of the meeting. In a sense, you will combine a meeting with a lunch, and the rest of the day is free.

7. Provide advance handouts on some of the items on the agenda, especially low-priority items that might be inadequately covered at the meeting.

8. Prioritize the items that need to be discussed. If the last item has to be dropped because of time constraints, then little is lost, because it wasn't that important anyway. You can table it until the next meeting.

9. Check the environment for the meeting, including:
   • Sufficient seating
   • Signs indicating the location of the meeting
   • Audio-visual equipment in place and in working order
   • Any outside events that could affect the scheduling or the location

10. Be prepared to have post-meeting handouts or mailings that summarize the proceedings and perhaps include an evaluation form.

The 12 Most Popular Sales Meeting Training Topics

A cross-section of national sales organizations was given a list of 59 sales training topics and asked to rate them on their overall merit. The results are as follows:

Effective listening	34 percent
Closing sales and gaining commitment	32
Maintaining self-motivation	27
Managing time	25
Making cold calls	24
Dealing with clients who say "no"	23
Making presentations	23
Opening calls	22
Strategic questioning	22
Selling against price	21
Asking questions	21
Problem-solving selling	19

What salespeople prefer as training topics are not necessarily the best topics, even if they are popular ones. Current thinking leans more toward emphasizing partnerships between buyers and sellers.

The *Forum's Selling in the 1990s: A Sales Productivity Report* suggests that salespeople need to consider themselves "integral to their employers' bottom line success...responsible not just for sales volume, but for profitability."

Successful salespeople, according to the report, now play many different roles. Sales training programs should be broad enough to include such items as:

- Avoiding adversarial relationships
- Establishing joint ventures and strategic alliances with customers
- Acting as coordinators and resource managers
- Assuming the role of local territory marketers

- Establishing and maintaining a few key accounts
- Becoming strategists who can look at the customer's customers
- Evaluating competitors' roles and acting as information channels for the home office
- Thinking "telemarketing" to reduce direct contact costs
- Assuming the role of confidant to customers, understanding their goals, problems, and concerns

Humor in Humility—At a Sales Meeting

A lesson in humility was driven home at a recent sales meeting. The divisional sales manager enjoyed using negative feedback. He believed that it produced better results. When low sales and profitability figures were reported for the second time, he came down pretty hard on the assembled reps.

"I've had enough excuses from you guys. If you can't do the job, perhaps there are others who would jump at the chance to represent our brand," he told the group. Then, pointing to a recently recruited man, a former NFL football player, he asked, "If a team isn't winning, what happens? The players are replaced—right?"

The question hung heavily in the air for a few seconds, but then the ex-football player said slowly, "Actually, boss, if the whole team was having trouble, we usually got a new coach."

Introducing Sales Presentation Aids and How to Use Them

If your sales team uses some kind of sales aid in customer presentations, the sales meeting is an excellent place to introduce new or revised ones. It is also an excellent opportunity to discuss ways to use these aids. Above all, the meeting opens the door to conduct some training. You could plan a demonstration, rehearse it prior to the meeting, and then have the sales team practice on each other.

The show-and-tell game of selling is very tempting. But will everyone on your sales team deem it appropriate at all times? Experience and common sense will often offer answers, but they might not coincide with yours. A checklist will help give some direction to your roundtable discussions with your team.

Just remember that the customer to whom they will demonstrate their expertise with a sales aid wants two major things: He or she wants to be listened to and to find out what's new in the shortest possible time.

Sales staff also need to be reminded to give the customer at least equal time in the presentation and not to let the glitter of a sales aid presentation get in the way. Sales aids are only support tools that should clarify a sales presentation, dramatize it, and lend it visual credibility.

Jack Falvey suggests you ask yourself and your sales team eight questions:

1. Will the sales aids contribute to my sales presentation instead of interfere with it?

2. Are the sales aids flexible enough to be used in different sales situations?

3. Are the sales aids high quality, and do they reflect my expertise and do our product or service proud?

4. Is the technological format their chief advantage or do the sales aids really convey what we want them to?

5. Are you—or your sales reps—familiar with the sales aids and comfortable using them?

6. Do the sales reps use your sales aids voluntarily, recognizing their value, or do you need to make their use compulsory?

7. Are the sales aids easy and quick to use or do they take an inordinate amount of time to work with?

8. Are the sales aids customer friendly or do they tend to intimidate customers?

Because your company spends a great deal of time and money on sales aids, all of these questions should have positive answers. If not, you could be wasting time and your company's money. Their value also depends on your product or service. If the product is a self-explanatory "star of the show," perhaps your salespeople don't need as much gift wrapping.

Sales aids are expensive, but they are most expensive if your sales reps do not use them or if they misuse them. The sales meeting is an excellent place to train your sales team in how and when sales aids should be used.

The Psychological Impact of Effective Meetings

There is more to running a successful meeting than meets the eye. Some corporate executives still maintain a fraternity party mentality, and sales managers, trying to please, often go along with putting on juvenile shows. The more serious meeting planners have veered away from uniform shirts and gag gifts.

Sales meetings have a different purpose. Be sure to check with your controller or CFO to make sure the projected expenses for the meeting are tax deductible.

Ten Items to Consider Before Your Next Sales Meeting

1. **Show business**—Is the sales meeting an assembly of professionals or is it an exercise in show business? Do you want to run an adolescent summer camp or try to accomplish a serious sales goal?

2. **Full-day meetings**—Attending a full-day meeting is different from putting in a full day of making sales calls. The audience is for the most part interested in learning how to improve those sales calls, and only short stretches of speeches and training are effective. Full-day meetings are usually found to be counterproductive.

3. **Awards and recognition**—If you are planning a meeting that will last for several days and awards or recognition will be given, schedule them for the first evening, when everyone will be present and alert.

4. **Half-day meetings**—If you are running a formal program, schedule it for half a day. The returns on a morning half-day program far exceed what you get if the program stretches into the post-lunch hours.

5. **Speakers**—Speakers as well as coaches know when their audiences are at a peak. A basketball team on a road trip invariably

performs better on Wednesday and Thursday than on Friday. On Friday, their minds are on packing and going back home.

6. **Dress**—Dress has a psychological component. The audience can be dressed casually, but the presenter needs to be more professional, and dress should match the serious purpose at hand. This depends, of course, on the type and purpose of the event.

7. **Resort hotels**—Temptations at sales conferences, especially if held in a resort setting, can be destructive. Levity can send the wrong message to the attendees. Sales managers and meeting planners should subtly remind the audience that more sales reps have been fired for inappropriate conduct at meetings than for any other reason other than non-performance.

8. **Meeting theme and objectives**—What message do you want your audience to receive? You need to be clear about your own objectives before you can direct others to follow them.

9. **Trade shows with sales meetings**—Trade shows and sales meetings? They are difficult to justify in terms of time and expense. Trade shows can be informative, but they are tiring affairs and usually don't mix well with the purposes of a sales meeting. Personnel who have the experience, time, and stamina should attend trade shows separately.

10. **Meeting length**—As far as meetings go, shorter is usually better. Although it is a difficult job to cut your meeting plans down to manageable size, it must be done. In this case, less can be more.

One company invited a number of its best customers to address a sales meeting. Hearing about the objectives and plans of the very people on whom your fortunes depend can be a crucial educational experience. It is also great public relations.

Environmental Awareness—Ten Pointers for a "Greener" Sales Meeting

Environmental issues are affecting all industries. As a sales manager, you can seize this issue and turn it into an opportunity. The Lenox Hotel in Boston compiled a list of ten pointers for a "greener" meeting.

1. Establish clear environmental guidelines long before your sales meeting takes place.

2. Whenever possible, use recycled paper for your exhibits and promotional materials. Print all handouts and other written material on both sides of each page.

3. Find unique, environmentally sound giveaways for your company, such as recycled plastic mugs, reusable cloth bags, or items of clothing made from cotton or recycled plastics.

4. Check to see if the meeting facility has a recycling program for materials such as paper, cardboard, wooden pallets, cans, and bottles. Tell your salespeople how to recycle their leftover materials.

5. Create exhibits, sales aids, and other materials that can be re-used. The investment will save you both dollars and resources.

6. Consider decorating ideas that exclude helium-filled balloons. They often end up floating in the ocean, where they are mistaken for food by turtles and whales. Instead, create a decor using flowers, rented greenery, or streamers.

7. Pack appropriate meeting materials in shredded office paper instead of bubble wrap or polystyrene pellets. Produce only the amount of distribution material that is really needed.

8. Schedule "fresh-air breaks" during the meeting, and suggest a walk in a nearby park. Encourage participants to use public transportation whenever possible.

9. Collect plastic name badges and reuse them at future meetings.

10. Communicate your ideas to your salespeople with a series of daily environmental reminders. Add a section to your sales meeting evaluation form asking everyone for more "green" suggestions for future meetings.

If Your Sales Meeting Is an Annual Affair

Wilner & Associates has planned and conducted numerous sales meetings over the past years. Drawing from a cornucopia of experience, a blueprint has evolved. Annual sales meetings serve many purposes, including the following:

Motivation—Schedule a time to give out awards (recognition for special achievements, contest winners, etc.). This is also an opportunity for the high-performing salespeople and sales managers to "tell 'em how they did it." Inspirational sales-oriented speakers also play a useful role in motivation.

Information exchange—The meeting is a time to deliver the status of sales results compared to the plan for the preceding year, review plans for the year ahead, and reveal the new merchandising, advertising, and promotion plans. Merchandise managers unveil their new product line strategies. Salespeople can be a rich source of competitive intelligence and feedback for personnel at company headquarters.

Social—The meeting is a time to rekindle old friendships, to rub elbows with company executives in an informal setting, and to get to know other staff, such as merchandise and product managers, customer service, technical support, manufacturing, and credit personnel.

Expensive—The cost of national sales meetings is sometimes staggering. Travel, hotels, meals, and entertainment are obvious costs, but the real major cost is the time spent by those participating, especially the sales staff who aren't making order-producing sales calls.

Opportunity for training—The national sales meeting is frequently neglected as an opportunity to conduct efficient sales training. Hotel, travel, and recreational arrangements—plus preparing executives' and specialists' internal presentations—frequently absorb the lion's share of planning for the event. But a sales meeting is a golden opportunity to train the sales organization about products, new selling strategies, or even "back-to-basics" fundamentals. However, in order to make training pay off for meeting planners, some fundamental concepts must be considered.

Summary of Fundamental Concepts

Sales meetings can be successful if they follow some simple, fundamental concepts:

1. Establish a clear set of objectives. Write them down, and consider what you want the participants to:

- Learn
- Experience
- Feel as a result of participating in the sales meeting

2. Look for areas in which your salespeople need training, such as:
   - Handling customer objections
   - Introducing a new advertising or promotion program
   - Presenting a new incentive merchandising campaign
   - Reinforcement of recent training completed
   - Selling by using a sales proposal
   - Selling into a new distribution channel
   - Selling to major accounts
   - Sales presentation (general line or new product introduction)
   - Time and territory management

3. Involve field sales management in determining training needs.

4. Write up typical "cases" that provide a real-world basis for the new skills or knowledge you want the salespeople to acquire.

5. Advise salespeople ahead of time that they will be part of a team, and let them know what they will be expected to do (tell a success story, make a feature/benefit presentation, write a proposal, solve a problem, etc.).

6. Put someone who is skilled in training, speaking, and adult learning in charge of the training portion of your meeting.

7. Allow plenty of time for this important learning experience (items 5 and 6 above), at least three hours.

8. Make the exercise competitive. Have participants judge themselves, and provide an award for each winning team member.

9. Make subject matter experts available for consultation during the meeting.

10. Make the training experience as important as the physical facilities, food, entertainment, and recreation.

11. Involve field sales management in active follow-up after the sales meeting.

Including a current, hard-hitting training experience in your next national or regional sales meeting can have a high payoff. Paying attention to fundamentals will ensure this happens.

Sales Meeting Countdown

Schedule for more cost-effective, productive sales meetings:

Days	Action to Be Taken	By Whom	Date Completed
–365	• Set meeting date	VP Sales	
	• Select a meeting site (See checklist below)	VP Sales	
–120	• Request input from everyone in sales department on meeting theme, agenda, wants, marketing or sales thrust, and timing	VP Sales	
	• Investigate hotel details—sleeping and meeting room needs	VP Sales	
–90	• Establish theme; everyone involved in meeting begins building materials around theme	VP Sales	
	• Meet with marketing, design, or merchandising to blend wants and answers to key questions	VP Sales	
	• Confirm any outside speakers or trainers	VP Sales	
–60	• Finalize meeting objectives	VP Sales	
	• Review marketing/sales thrust, theme, objectives, sales skill language, and outlines for presentations	VP Sales	
	• Confirm hotel details (number of sleeping and meeting rooms, food, and various events)	VP Sales	
	• Announce sales meeting to sales force and all concerned	VP Sales	
	• Provide instructions to all presenters (i.e., time allotted, theme, objectives, etc.)	VP Sales	
–60	• Conduct interviews with senior management and other key influencers who will be presenting	VP Sales	

Days	Action to Be Taken	By Whom	Date Completed
–45	• Develop questionnaire for sales-people and distribute to all	VP Sales	
	• Develop draft agenda	VP Sales	
–30	• Salespeople return completed questionnaire to their sales managers	All	
	• Update presentation outlines	All	
	• Review room setups, audio-visual equipment, meal and refreshment needs	VP Sales	
	• Mail any pre-read assignments to salespeople	VP Sales	
–15	• Set up meeting flow so each breakout session builds on meeting theme and last discussion	VP Sales	
	• Rehearsal of all presentations (look for marketing thrust, theme, and sales skill language)	VP Merch.	
	• Analyze questionnaires tabulated by sales managers	VP Sales	
	• Generate summary report	VP Sales	
	• Develop and send to meeting site list of arrangements that must be made	VP Sales	
–15	• Review and complete meeting evaluation questionnaire	VP Sales	

Meeting

- Distribute summary report of questionnaire.
- Arrange to collect key concerns and action items generated in each breakout session.
- Set up a task force to address concerns and action items.
- Collect meeting evaluation questionnaires.

Post-Meeting

- At the meeting site, hold a brief evaluation meeting with all sales managers and planners of the meeting.
- Review the following questions with the group:
  1. Was the primary objective accomplished?
  2. Was the agenda adequate or too long?
  3. Did the meeting start and end on time?
  4. Was the audience interested and attentive?
  5. Did the audience leave in an upbeat mood?
  6. Were we all prepared?
  7. Were appropriate visuals used by all presenters?
  8. Were there any problems with the visuals?
  9. Did we stay within budget?
  10. Were the meeting rooms satisfactory?
  11. Did we implement our environmental guidelines? If so, how?
  12. Were there any problems with meals or refreshments?
  13. Was there adequate participation by the salespeople?

Checklist for Selecting a Sales Meeting Site

- Is the location easy to travel to?
- Are the rates within your budget?
- Are the sleeping accommodations clean and comfortable?
- Are the meeting rooms adequate in size, lighting, and ventilation?
- Is the food available both appetizing and good quality?
- Is the facility staff helpful and friendly?
- Are the chairs comfortable?
- Will necessary audio-visual equipment be available?
- Is the facility interested in environmental issues?
- Is there adequate parking?
- Are references available from previous users?

Sales meetings skillfully planned and executed can be very valuable to a sales manager. There are many reasons for conducting a sales meeting. Motivating sales reps more effectively and achieving better results than could have be done on a one-on-one basis are basic reasons for competency in planning and leading a meeting. More important is the opportunity to display those essential leadership skills that were discussed in Chapter 3.

CHAPTER 13

The Electronic Office

Automation is a form of mechanization, an advanced stage of systematizing and simplifying work. Like all computer technology, automation is undergoing rapid change. It is typically applied to labor-intensive functions, such as tracking inventory, ordering merchandise, and maintaining communication between two distant points. In addition, there is now software that will keep track of your sales representatives' activities away from the office.

Typically, actual computer use by sales representatives can be grouped into three areas. According to a survey by the Professional Society of Sales and Marketing Training, the percentage of usage in these areas was:

1. Call presentation preparation—38 percent
2. Collection and recording of sales call data—34 percent
3. Use during the sales call—28 percent

In the September 1996 issue of *Selling Power,* Paul Selden, president of the Sales Automation Association, recommended considering each aspect of the sales cycle as candidates for automation in order to achieve maximum return on your technology investment:

1. Getting leads
2. Screening leads
3. Making initial appointments
4. Analyzing prospect/customer needs

5. Estimating product and cost response
6. Validating response with technical staff
7. Preparing proposals
8. Closing
9. Follow-up for later sales
10. Servicing customers

Automation using notebook computers can reduce the time it takes to correspond, fill orders, relay instructions, and travel back and forth from the field to headquarters. Many companies are abandoning the age-old daily sales report in favor of a faster, computer-based data collection and information system.

It can be expensive to computerize a sales team. The cost can be as much as $10,000 to $15,000 per salesperson for complete technology support. Although equipment is costly, costs are steadily going down as more equipment is being manufactured and used. Computerization also requires training in how to use a notebook (handheld) computer. This involves a detailed "needs analysis" of what you and your people know and do not know about both the computer and software to be used. Then the training can be custom-designed on how to proficiently use and operate your computer system. However, the end result is saving money—which improves the bottom line of companies hard-pressed by spiraling sales costs.

If a sales representative's territory is 1000 miles from the central office, returning for meetings, instructions, training and processing orders could cost $500 to $1,000. Moreover, the sales rep's absence from his or her territory and customers could result in a reduction in services and sales, which could amount to thousands of dollars. The cost of one trip could pay for a notebook computer.

As the sales rep's functions are being automated in increasing numbers, home offices are being automated even more quickly. Office and clerical work that supports a sales rep's efforts has always been notable for low productivity. Labor-intensive hand operations in the home office are now giving way to automation.

In this context, automation devices include high-speed desktop computers that can handle electronic mail (internal e-mail and external Internet mail), voice message systems, high-speed phone systems, cellular phones, portable fax machines, electronic filing, personal workstations, automated inventory records, and much more.

TeleProfessional magazine's May 1994 issue included an article on how inside sales and field sales are working in tandem with other sales and marketing elements. The article, "Advances in Sales Automation Technology Fuel Rise in Team Selling Concept," described how increased technological sophistication is helping the "dream" of true inside/outside team selling become a reality.

Sales Management of the Future

Today's sales directors will have to take advantage of mobile environments. *Mobile* refers to the nearly 25 million sales reps whom we call the "road warriors" of business. They rarely go into their offices, yet they need to communicate with headquarters and interact with managers and others on the team.

Electronic interaction is needed on a global scale. Sales managers need to think globally, as even small companies are increasingly expanding into international sales. Automation equipment is now on hand to make worldwide contact a reality on every level. Automation equipment (multimedia notebook computers) will enable your sales team to:

- Make more time for selling by using a calendar and a weekly itinerary, and by producing daily sales reports with appropriate scheduling software programs that can be sent to headquarters via e-mail
- Expand their reach through ticklers, use of customer form letters, and an increased prospect file
- Increase opportunities to close by having immediate access to your host system while they are out on the road
- Process orders faster and more efficiently
- Check sales and credit and payment histories minutes before a sales call as well as afterward
- Access inventories, prices, and delivery schedules from their cars, hotel rooms, or the customers' offices
- Access on-line engineering or configuration programs and generate anticipated "what-if" scenarios
- Use dual fax capabilities to contact either the home office or other customers

- Confirm signatures required for pharmaceutical sales
- Work with spreadsheets, proposals, and accounting or customer data while on the road and working with a customer
- Use e-mail messages from any location, 24 hours a day, to communicate with their sales manager, other salespeople, and customers
- Transmit letters, memos, and orders to the home or district office instantaneously
- Transmit information about:
  - Product failures
  - Non-deliveries
  - Competitive intelligence
  - Home office support requests
  - Product/service suggestions

And they will be able to do all this instantaneously, thus increasing a company's capacity to react quickly.

With 37 million men and women expected to work outside their offices by the end of the decade, automation is fast becoming necessary for the modern sales manager.

The downsizing and reengineering of companies and the greater emphasis on enhancing the bottom line make automation the white knight for our road warriors. Tom Villani of NCR says, "The electronic cord has been cut. Now when there's a need to instantly gain access to critical data, you can."

David Grimes, a vice president of the Business Communication Services division of AT&T, managed a sales force in a ten-state area. Grimes decided that the way to control rising administrative costs and increase revenue in his division was to equip his sales force with portable notebook computers. This automation would make home office visits unnecessary.

Within two years, Grimes was able to free up 90 support people to accept new assignments elsewhere in the company. His 300-member sales staff has significantly increased its "face time." They see and sell to more customers, are able to access office files for preparation of sales presentations, and can review customers' purchase and service records. They also send and receive electronic mail messages and faxes from their cars, airport lounges, or customers' offices.

The bottom line is that Grimes has eliminated 50 percent of peripheral expense. The sales force's newfound freedom enables it to do what it does best—sell. Productivity went up an average of 45 percent.

Reviewing Grimes's success, one of NCR's marketing managers, Tom Villani, commented, "People are working flextime, sharing jobs, or working out of their homes, and they need (electronic) systems to stay in touch. It's basically a competitive weapon. These days, if you can't get to needed information quickly, your competition will, and that means they will come in and clean your clock."

The truly mobile sales team is just beginning to become a reality. Innovations are just breaking through the limitations of sales management. Today's restrictions are like the speed at which we can travel to distant planets or the batteries that allow us only limited mobility with electric cars. In another decade or two, we will approach speeds that can send our astronauts all over the galaxy and produce electric cars that aren't bound to nightly energy outlets.

Portable or notebook computers will soon have radio talk capabilities. "Internet Talk Radio" is now available, not just to scientists but to sales managers who want to be in voice contact with their representatives and consumers. "Internet: Info Highway Shortcut Snares More Business," the business section cover story in the July 7, 1994 edition of *USA Today,* describes the way firms like Joe Boxer plug in to pitch products and solve problems. They have dropped their toll-free numbers and started relying on the Internet to reach customers. Face-to-face contact via small screens will come right behind this latest electronic marvel.

Data will be storable and played later or reviewed after a day's selling activity. Paul Saffo, a computer industry analyst at the Institute for the Future in Menlo Park, California, believes that a global radio network via computers "is pregnant with possibilities." Fiber-optic circuits will make such face-to-face communication a reality.

In a way, the future seems to indicate that desktop broadcasting is just around the corner. Can desktop sales management be far behind?

Future Shock

Future salespeople and managers growing up in this decade will take tomorrow's innovations for granted, but the vast number of older "road warrior" professionals will be astounded by what is now being developed and what will be in use by the year 2000.

There has been much talk about artificial intelligence (AI). It is sometimes called neuro-network technology because it works something like the human brain. An article on AI appeared in the January 1993 issue of *Sales & Marketing Management* magazine. The article detailed how today's salespeople use AI software systems to help resolve complex sales situations. These systems can determine the most qualified prospects, the most applicable sales methods, and the most effective way to solve customers' problems. "Product-matching systems," according to the the article, will help salespeople deliver the best solutions to their customers' needs."

Another future benefit is the international standardization of software—including electronic mail, communications, and electronic data interchange (EDI). This will allow information to be passed between different vendors, providing a framework in which software developers can design products that work with those of other vendors.

Pad and tablet computers, already on the market, will also develop greater utility and sophistication. Miniaturization will continue until convertibility, pocket-size tablets, and pen or finger activation become commonplace.

Several classes of pad or tablet computers are currently being developed, including:

- General-purpose tablets
- Convertible pen computers
- Minitablet pen computers
- Megatablet pen computers
- Multimodal megatablets
- Special-purpose data entry and data collection tablets

Cellular communication is available and will grow, encompassing both voice and data capabilities. Recent advances in handheld cellular phones and modem technology and an expanding cellular network will make cellular communication a potentially powerful sales automation tool.

The more practical application of cellular communication will enable salespeople to send and receive data anytime, anywhere, providing higher levels of customer service and satisfaction.

We can also look forward to substantial cost reductions in this equipment. Even within the next two or three years, wireless communication products and their usage fees are expected to drop by at least one-half of current rates. Despite the expected price reduction, quality will increase. Wireless networks will improve, and coverage areas will increase.

Videophones, which now cost around $1,000, will come into greater use as prices are reduced through greater production and number of sending and receiving stations.

Multimedia is another term we hear in sales automation. It is the blending of several technologies—such as voice, sound, video, still images, monochromatic and multicolor graphics, and traditional computer applications. The current generation of notebooks have some of these multimedia facilities, and more will be developed to make them even more versatile.

Software will probably undergo the most dramatic changes. A new software programming technique called "object orientation" will have the greatest impact on the software products and application systems of the future. Object orientation is based on the concept of breaking software programs into components or "objects" which are reusable with other programs. Object-oriented systems are supposedly easier to understand and easier to program once an object-oriented foundation has been established. They are also easier to maintain and upgrade—especially as business environments change.

According to *Sales & Marketing Management* magazine, "in the long-run, companies adopting object-oriented sales automation systems enjoy lower costs of ownership and a faster payback on their investment."

Pass the Laptop, Please!

A funny thing was observed on a Southern beach. A youngish executive and his family have themselves comfortable under a folding beach canopy. When they were oiled up and settled, the man asked his wife to pass him a compact case, which he opened and converted into a battery-operated laptop computer.

While this scenario might seem like an extreme example of "getting away from it all," it is more prevalent than one might suppose. *INC.* magazine's fall 1992 FaxPoll reported that while 98 percent of executive respondents used computers in the office and 76 percent used them at home, 12 percent actually took a portable version to the beach or into the mountains with them.

Automation is here to stay. To keep up, here's what you can do:

- Investigate the needs of your sales force.
- Find out what other companies your size are doing.

- Determine what your budget is for hardware and then software.
- Plan for changes in information needs or system design. It is inevitable. The system you buy will need modification.
- Utilize your management information systems department early on to help assess your needs and how quickly modifications can be made when you need them.
- Conduct a test with a couple of your best salespeople.
- Streamline your reports—keep it simple (KIS). Only include the "must-know" information for your sales team. Too much of a good thing is bad!
- Provide your own manual for your salespeople in their language. Computer manuals are much too technical and difficult to understand for many people.
- Read:
  o *The Internet Business Guide* by Rosalind Resnick and Dave Taylor, Sams Publishing, 1994.
  o "Virtual Selling," *INC.,* Technology Issue, Vol. 16, No. 13, pages 61–71.
  o "The User Guide to Sales, Customer Service, and Marketing Automation," Information Systems Marketing (phone: 202 363-8996).

Also read business magazines like *INC., Entrepreneur, Selling Power, Sales & Marketing Management,* and *Fortune* that feature updated articles, resources, and case histories not usually found in sales management and trade-specific journals.

Each year, *Sales & Marketing Management* includes in its December issue a PC-based sales and marketing applications software directory. Recently, 40 pages listed 400 vendors and nearly 500 packages that range across 23 categories. The December 1993 listings were limited to those packages that specifically help sales managers perform their jobs more proficiently.

CHAPTER 14

Humor and Storytelling in Selling and Managing

> The storyteller in the fullness of his craft has struck, and the spell is on...
>
> Melvin Maddocks, *Time* magazine

The fairy tales you listened to as a child often began with "Once upon a time." A bit stilted, a little dull, nevertheless the phrase was always a handy device to open a story. Many of us still use it when we tell stories to our own children and grandchildren.

Once upon a time, the storytelling, cigar-chomping salesman was an archetypal visitor to every store in the country. There was not a story, anecdote, or joke that he didn't know and couldn't pull out to fit a particular sales situation.

It would be a shame if this talent were to go to waste. But that's not likely because today's customers aren't that different. Humor still has a place in salesmanship, but it has become more sophisticated and more pertinent to the product or service.

The technique of using humor and storytelling to embellish a sales proposal is unlikely to go out of fashion. Between the bolts and nuts, and bytes and roms, is still that old-fashioned human element—the smile. And a smile, accompanied by a relevant story, coats any sales talk with infallible lubricant.

The light touch, as many an old-timer can tell you, can have heavy results. The proverbial old-time salesmen used this technique unabashedly. They used it so much that they became the caricatured victim of their own technique. Today, we use motivation, empathy, and pop psychology, but humor and storytelling still satisfy the human need for enjoyment, entertainment, and pertinence.

Experienced account executives still use anecdotes that contain elements of humor and which are also well-thought-out stories that illustrate and enhance the product and service. This helps prospects relax and turns them into customers. Empathy, a way of creating rapport or "good vibes" with a sales prospect, has taken the place of the slap on the back. Knowledge has replaced the cigar.

When you sell with stories, you allow the customer to walk onto a stage with you—a stage where you set up the props and you direct the action.

Random storytelling that has no point or is not pertinent to the business at hand is actually a distraction. It becomes an ego trip for the story-teller and can bore the customer right out of a sales decision. It is vital, therefore, that anecdotes and any type of humor used in a sales situation have relevancy to the product or service being demonstrated or presented.

This basic and pragmatic fact applies to salesmanship as well as other forms of marketing. Direct mail and advertising can also suffer from the same destructive influence of impertinent and non-essential storytelling.

> Small jokes are more effective than big jokes when making a business speech (or presentation). A joke that delivers big laughs may distract the audience from the business point you are trying to make. A small joke that illustrates a point reinforces the message.
>
> —Michael Iapoce,
> Communications Consultant, San Anselmo, California

Let's look at an example of a pertinent story. Suppose you are the sales manager for a large liquor distributor. Your salespeople call on dozens of retail liquor dealers in a four-state area. One thing they don't need is temperance. While it would be bad psychology to advocate drunkenness, a sly reference to the temperance movement may be well received by the customer, especially if the story is attributed to a famous, highly regarded person.

Here's how the story goes. Winston Churchill once christened a new Royal Navy ship with the traditional bottle of champagne. A representative from the Women's Christian Temperance Union rebuked the prime minister and suggested that he had set a bad example by using an alcoholic beverage to launch a ship. The prime minister shifted his cigar to the other side of his mouth, looked the lady straight in the eye, and said, "Madam, it is traditional that a ship takes its first sip of wine and then proceeds on water ever after."

The story is relevant to the business at hand. It gets attention and paves the way for the next step—preparing the customer for the subject that interests him most, in this case, the brand of liquor you are pushing at the moment. On the other hand, if you feel uncomfortable using such a story, by all means leave it out.

If you can't find a pertinent story, you can always resort to an anecdote about a desirable attribute, such as quality. Again Winston Churchill comes to the rescue. Before he was expected in New York for a visit, the manager of the hotel where he would be staying asked the British embassy representative about Mr. Churchill's taste in food and wine. "Oh," answered the embassy representative, "the prime minister really has quite simple tastes. He is always satisfied with the best." At this juncture you can point out that your company has taken this lesson to heart by producing only the best quality product.

It is much better to get a point across without seeming to brag. A short story that takes half a minute to tell will make the quality pitch much more agreeable and credible.

You may at some point find yourself called upon to give a speech in a non-sales situation. This can be one of life's frightening moments or it can be a joyous occasion that your audience will remember. Pick out a little story that shows your humility.

When speakers poke a little fun at themselves, it is always well-received. And if they can flatter the audience, they have created the kind of empathy that creates applause and approval. Here's an example:

> When I was a young man, I left the farm and came to the big city to make my fame and fortune in sales. The farm's loss was the city's gain. But into sales I got, and it wasn't always easy for a rube from the sticks. At the beginning of my career, I was selling hats. I walked into a store in a small Pennsylvania town and got ready to make my spiel about the high quality of my hats. The owner picked up one I had just touted at $10 wholesale. He looked me straight in the eye and said, "Where are the holes in the hat?" Flustered, I answered, "But there aren't any holes in the hat." The storekeeper replied, "Why, there must

be—only a jackass would pay ten bucks for this hat, so it's gotta have two holes in it." So you see, the life of a salesman isn't always easy...

The use of stories in salesmanship does not come automatically. Even the great comics, whose humor appeared to come across almost accidentally, practiced and polished those "instantaneous" and oft-quoted retorts. Will Rogers, Jack Benny, Myron Cohen—all of the great storytellers worked hard at producing the kind of stories that created empathy and enjoyment—and results. It's a good idea to keep a file on some sales areas applicable to your business that will help you create humor so that they are accessible to you.

Salesmanship, like other forms of persuasion, follows a fairly orderly and logical pattern, and lighthearted stories and humor help to enhance the process. The sales process used in one form or another to train salespeople consists of the following steps:

- Establishing rapport
- Assessing and establishing needs
- Presenting benefits/features
- Overcoming concerns
- Closing
- Following up

This sales process can be varied according to your buyer. Using it will help you achieve the objectives of the call.

- **Establishing rapport**—Tell a story, create empathy, or present a benefit using humor. Humor can be a great attention-getting device. It has been suggested that people initially have a ho-hum attitude when a speaker begins to talk to them. This frequently occurs with a customer or prospect, and rapport needs to be established before communication can take place. A popular way to go after attention is with a story, an incident, or an illustration that is humorous.

- **Assessing and establishing needs**—Assess your buyer's needs by asking high-gain questions.

- **Presenting benefits/features**—Match your product's benefits to the needs uncovered by using stories about your product, service, or process that your company has compiled over the years.

- **Overcoming concerns**—Overcome any concerns, skepticism, or drawbacks with testimonials, proof, lab reports, or stories.
- **Closing**—There is only one thing left to do—close. Ask for the order; and that, my friend, is no story.
- **Following up**—Make sure that what you sold is delivered on time as ordered. If you don't, you better have a good story to tell!

The World's Most Expensive Sales Promotion

Sadly, this story is about a great sales promotion that worked too well. The result was what its creators had intended, and it is absolutely true.

Early in 1993, the European division of the staid Maytag Company of Newton, Iowa, (its name is Hoover Limited) was asked to come up with a promotion to get consumers to buy the company's electric appliances and vacuum cleaners again. The sales manager came up with the bright idea of offering a free trip to a number of destinations in Europe and the United States to any customer who purchased Hoover products for $150 to $375.

The results were just short of spectacular. Appliances sold like proverbial hotcakes. The only problem was that the cost of the promotion was too high, and free trips could not be awarded fast enough to accommodate a quarter of a million buyers. The results were:

1. Nearly 200,000 dissatisfied customers waiting for their free trips
2. A $48,800,000 cost that had to be charged against first-quarter earnings
3. The president of Hoover Europe, who had authorized this fiasco, and his two sales managers were fired

Lighten Up!

"It's not coincidental that the most successful people are those who combine good business and a sense of humor," said Patrick Townsend, a Holden, Massachusetts, author and quality advisor. Townsend claims that losing your sense of humor has a negative effect on business.

Failing to lighten up to the humorous side of life, especially in today's hectic business world, can cause unnecessary stress. In sales, we often encounter situations with customers and prospects that border on being catastrophic. Actually, they can be rather amusing when we think about them in retrospect. True, we might have to look hard to find the humor, but if we look, chances are we'll find it.

At your next sales or training meeting, keep your eyes open for some funny incidents and adopt or create some slogans. Then, tack up a few of the slogans that will make the attendees smile. You'll probably notice that some of them jot them down for their own use. It's also a great way to get them on your side.

Here are some examples:

> Humor is a universal language. You'll need no interpreter.

> A joke is a very serious thing. Use it judiciously.

> A smile is the shortest distance between two people.

> Life is too serious to be taken seriously.

> Humor is one of man's greatest natural resources. It can make sales as well as prevent wars with equal ease.

> If it ain't fun, it ain't worth doing.

> Seven days without laughter makes one weak.

> Humor is counterbalance. Laughter need not be cut out of anything, since it improves everything.

> Suavis autem est, et vehementer saepe utilis jocus et facetiae.

Cicero said the last example 2,000 years ago; it means: "Joking and humor are pleasant, and often of exceptional utility."

A Storytelling Starter Set

Collecting and building your own repertoire of stories offers a wonderful opportunity for:

- Team building
- Participatory management
- Employee involvement

Your salespeople will enjoy the process, especially if the results are made public and credited.

File ideas under a subject, so that you or anyone else can make use of them for specific, pre-planned occasions. You can collect ideas for sales presentations, sales meetings, or after-dinner speeches. Here are several stories to get you started.

Enthusiasm—A salesperson's excitement for the product or service can indeed be infectious. Enthusiasm, like persistence and product knowledge, is an ingredient of the sale, as exemplified in the following, possibly true, story about Harry Winston, the famed diamond merchant.

One day, Winston got a call from a wealthy Dutch collector, requesting to see a diamond in Winston's inventory. Winston assigned one of his best salesmen to the visitor, and the salesman launched into a description of the perfection of the stone. The prospective buyer was not sold and said he would have to think about it.

On his way out, Harry Winston stopped the visitor and asked whether he might show him the stone once more. The prospect agreed and Winston took him, and the diamond, into his office and proceeded to go on about his own love for diamonds and, in particular, his admiration for this historic gem. Within a short time, the Dutchman agreed to the purchase but asked Mr. Winston, as well as himself, "How come I bought this diamond from you, Mr. Winston, but not from your salesman?"

Winston smiled and answered, "That salesman is one of the best in the business. He probably knows more about diamonds than I do. But he *knows* diamonds—I *love* them!"

Humility—One day a big lion was stalking through the jungle, roaring at the top of his mighty voice, "Who is the king of the jungle?" A frightened zebra whispered: "You are, sir, you are." A chattering monkey said: "Oh, you are sir, yes sir."

Then a huge elephant came tromping through the bush, saw the lion, grabbed him with his trunk, and flung him into the trees. "Hey, man," cried the lion, "you don't have to get sore just because you don't know the answer!"

Insurance—An insurance agent talked to a prospective client at her home and noted an especially pretty vase on the mantle. He said, "What a gorgeous vase! Do you keep anything in it?" Said the lady, "Yes, my husband's ashes."

Answered the insurance agent: "Oh, I'm sorry. I didn't know he was deceased." He isn't," replied the woman. "He's just too lazy to hunt for an ashtray."

(Note that brevity is one of the charms of this little story. It takes no more than 30 seconds to tell.)

International trade—Wham-O, the company that makes frisbees, and its subsidiary, Kransco, joined an international charitable effort and shipped 7,000 of their popular plastic discs to an orphanage in Angola, West Africa, addressed to the attention of a nun named Sister Dominique.

A few weeks later, a letter arrived from the sister, addressed to the company's chairman, John Bowes. It read as follows: "The dishes you sent are wonderful. We eat all our meals from them. And the most amazing thing happened. Some of the children clean their plates diligently and then throw them around as sort of a game. This may be an idea for you!"

Listening—One of the sales manager and salesperson's greatest assets is an ability to listen. Salespeople listen to their prospect or customer's words—what they need, dream about, hope for. If you do too much talking, you will never have the opportunity to find out what your customer really wants and needs. The same applies to sales managers who must listen to their salespeople, who also have needs, dreams, careers, motivation, money, family, etc.

A story is told at Harvard University about a conversation between a professor and a female student. "Since there is no course in the art of conversation," the student said "how can I learn this?" "Certainly there is a way," the professor answered. "If you'll just listen, I'll tell you what it is."

Two minutes went by and the professor did not say a word. Finally the impatient student interrupted the long silence, "Well, I am listening."

"See," the professor said, "you're learning already."

Medical—A man in his seventies went to see a doctor after considerable urging from his family. "Doc, I know I am getting old, but I want to make sure that I live to be a hundred. Tell me how to do this," he said. The doctor immediately corrected the man: "Old is no longer the appropriate term. You are now considered chronologically endowed." Then the doctor asked, "Do you smoke?" "Nope." "Do you drink?" "Nary a drop." "Do you still fool around?" "Too dang much trouble." "Then why in the world do you want to live to a hundred?"

To emphasize the fact that the introduction of a new product requires considerable marketing and exposure to potential consumers, one sales manager told the following little story: A reporter once asked the prominent Texas Senator Alben W. Barkley, "What does it take to make a great senator?" "First," answered Barkley, "you've got to get elected."

Optician (also salesmanship)—An optometrist took his college grad son into the business. The first lesson he gave him was salesmanship. "After you've fitted the glasses," he preached, "and asked whether they are right, say, 'The charge is $50' and watch if the customer flinches. If not, pause a moment and say 'for the frames.' If the customer still isn't perturbed, add 'and the lenses are $10' and then pause again. If there's no reaction, add 'each'."

Real estate—A woman who is in the real-estate profession has a daughter who works for a dentist in her neighborhood. The dentist planned to sell his house/office and move into other facilities. The realtor got the listing.

She visited the dentist, who showed her through the building. The realtor took ample notes and prepared an ad for the newspaper, had it approved by the dentist, and ran it that weekend. The next weekend, she noticed that her ad appeared again, but with the dentist's own phone number.

The realtor asked her daughter to bring home an extracted tooth from the dentist's office. She tied the tooth to a note and sent it back to the dentist. The note read: "I did it myself. Thank you."

The dentist got the message—and the point—and the realtor got the listing back.

Retail—Jones & Smith was a popular hardware store in a northwestern city. Both partners had sons whom they hoped would take over the store one day. Jones's boy was working in the store when a customer bought a couple of tools that came to $5.99. The customer gave him a ten-dollar bill, and the young man handed it to his father, who happened to be at the cash register. To his surprise, Mr. Jones, Sr. found that two ten-dollar bills were stuck together. He found this to be a proper moment for some training for Junior.

"See this," said Jones, Sr., "two ten-dollar bills stuck together. This is where ethics comes in. Should I tell my partner or shouldn't I?"

Thinking big—A little boy's dog had several puppies. The boy wanted to sell one of them, so he stationed himself at a bus stop with a sign: "Dog for Sale—25 cents."

A neighbor salesman stopped by on the third day, and since the dog still hadn't sold, he said: "If you want to sell that dog, take him home, give him a bath, brush his coat, tie a blue ribbon on him, and raise that price!"

The boy did as the salesman suggested, and the next day his place at the bus stop was empty. The salesman, curious to see how his advice had worked, went to see the little boy and asked him how much he got for the puppy. The answer was $10,000.

The salesman was taken aback and said, "That's ridiculous. Nobody would pay $10,000 for a little dog. How in the world did you get $10,000 for it?" "Simple," said the boy. "I took two $5,000 cats for it!"

Time management—A trainer whose topic was On-Time Delivery told a story about a man who was cleaning out his parents' house after both of them had died. He found in the back of a drawer a shoe repair ticket that was 20 years old. The following day, out of curiosity, he went to the shoe repair shop. It was still there, and he gave the yellowed old ticket to the repairman. The repairman looked at it, turned it over, and then went to the back of the shop. In a minute he returned and said, "Your shoes will be ready Friday."

> There are three things which are real: God, human folly, and laughter. The first two are beyond our comprehension. So we must do what we can with the third.
>
> —John F. Kennedy

> Humor is serious business. It can serve as a powerful tool for leaders at all levels to prevent the build-up of stress, to improve communication, to enhance motivation and morale, to build relationships, to encourage creative problem solving, to smooth the way for organizational change, and to make workshops fun.
>
> —Joel Goodman, Director, The Humor Project

> Humor is essential to any smoothly functioning system of interaction, to any healthy person, and to any viable group. Humor is, in the last analysis, no joke.
>
> —Dr. Gary Alan Fine, University of Minnesota

Starting Your Own Humor Collection

If you are persuaded that humor has at least an occasional place in selling or sales management, you may have some questions about how to start:

- How do I start a humor collection?
- How do I remember the stories?
- Do I need to write my own?

More than a decade ago Charlie Herrmann, a great humorist and member of the Professional Society of Sales and Marketing Training, came up with some excellent answers to these questions in an editorial on humor which he wrote for unrestricted use by society members.

Taking the last question first, Charlie quoted comedy writer Robert Orben: "Humor users need not be humor creators. In fact, much of today's humor is acquired humor. The laugh maker extracts—from books, publications, services, and observation—one liners and stories that fit his or her personality and position. In time, a reservoir of instant and apt comedy response can be developed and drawn from as needed."

Jeannie Robertson, a "Funny Lady," as headlined in a profile article in the *Triad Business News* about her success as a professional speaker, says, "I'm always looking for a funny." Coming up with new humor, she believes, is key to her continued success, and that is why her trip journal is so important. On every speaking trip Jeannie tries to collect as many funny stories as possible. She asks cab drivers, airline attendants—just about anybody—to share a humorous story.

It is rewarding to develop what performers like Jeannie would call "a piece of material" that comes from experiences you've had, your imagination, your observations on life, and so forth. But the humor you use in managing your sales team or selling doesn't have to be original.

The following sources for humor are available to everyone:

1. **Your eyes**—Listen with your eyes. If you are alert, pay attention to what's going on around you, and if use your powers of observation, you'll record things for your humor file. Because of Charlie Herrmann's editorial, I became interested in automobile bumper stickers. There are many around, and some are very appealing. While driving in Seattle, I noticed one on a car in front of me: *The probability of someone watching you is directly proportional to*

the stupidity of your actions. I saw another favorite on the back of a plumber's truck: *A flush is better than a full house.* You see them on vehicles on highway and in parking lots and in specialty and gift shops. Many contain wise sayings or pertinent questions that revolve around issues of our times. These traveling observations are great fun to use in the appropriate sales or sales management situation. And don't forget the newspaper. You can use articles, columns, comic strips, political cartoons, and the sports section. One sports section headline read: "Complaints about NBA referees growing ugly."

2. **Your family, friends, neighbors, customers**—Your ears can be another great source for humor. Once people know that you have a need for stories, they will save them for you. When they see you, they may well open their conversation with "I've got a story for you." Listen to them, and when you hear a "keeper," write it down or put it into your computer. You will only get stories if you ask, "Have you heard any good stories lately?"

3. **Your television set**—Depending on the kind of humor you like, there are all kinds of talk show programs, specials, and other events that to be successful require great quantities of humor. It may take a little extra time, but if you are willing to watch television with legal pad close at hand, you can jot down the lines and stories that appeal to you most. Sometimes, there is a live audience to confirm or deny your judgment about what you think is funny. You don't need to immediately use the things you hear on television. Let the material age for a while in one of your files. As you may have noticed, the audience reaction is frequently favorable even when the story is old. Most people don't remember stories and jokes and don't mind hearing those they like again.

4. **Your library and bookstore rack**—There are numerous magazines, books, trade journals, collections of wit, humorous writings, children's books, and clip art that can provide excellent material. A trip through your library or book store's "humor" shelves can be a stimulating discovery. One book is among my favorites and I often refer to it: *A Funny Thing Happened on the Way to the Boardroom,* written by Michael Iapoce, is an excellent source of material that is more than

just a listing of jokes. You can get ideas on how to write one-liners and stories for your particular audience. When I am in the library, I always browse through the periodical *Vital Speeches.* There is often an interesting story by another speaker that can be adapted to a sales situation.

5. **Subscribe to a service**—There are a number of services you can subscribe to that will provide you with new and fresh material. Not all of what you get is usable, but each month I always seemed to find a few things that I could use and adapt to my audience. Here are a few sources:

   • Mack McGinnis, 448 Mitchner Ave., Indianapolis, IN 46219 (phone: 317-356-4616)
   • "HUMOResources," available from The Humor Project, 110 Spring Street, Saratoga Springs, NY 12866 (phone: 518-587-8770, fax: 800-600-4242)
   • Funny Filler, published monthly by the GROMA Corp., 656 Pearl Street, Suite 200, La Jolla CA 92037 (phone: 619-454-6626)
   • Capitol Comedy, ERP, P.O. Box 25605, Washington, DC 20007-8605 (phone: 301-881-8717)
   • Quote, The Speakers Digest, 1627 Peachtree Street, Suite 302, Atlanta, GA 30309 (phone: 404-881-6811, 404-881-8835)

6. **Nightclubs, entertainment events, and other speakers**—Borrowing a couple of lines that your favorite entertainer or other presenters use is perfectly acceptable. However, it is important that you give credit to your source by saying, "As Jeanne Robertson tells it..." or "Joan Rivers contends that..." or "Zig Ziglar tells a story about..." etc.

It is important to note that while humor can lighten and enlighten a sales or sales management situation, it may not be appropriate in every situation. The sensitive communicator should weigh the pros and cons in every situation. In the February 1992 issue of *Meetings and Conventions* magazine, comedy writer Robert Orben said: "If you're sold on the use of humor in communication, beware of the tendency to be oversold."

Do's and Don'ts of Humor

Here are a few do's and don'ts of humor:

Don't try too hard	Be natural/unpredictable
Don't expect hilarity	Chuckles are okay
Don't backpedal	Move on after you tell your story
Don't attack	If in doubt, leave it out
Don't wing it	Research and prepare

Humor, Comedy, and Wit

So far we have made no attempt to define what humor is. Steve Allen once wrote, "Humor is surprise." Jeanne Robertson points out that she is a humorist, not a comedian, and says: "Comedians really go after the jugular; they throw out one-liners, and their only purpose is to get the majority of the audience to laugh." James Thurber defined humor as "emotional chaos remembered in tranquillity."

A humorist paints the picture with words so that the people in the audience will say, "I have been there, too." If I tell stories about my selling days and talk about a difficult customer I handled in a humorous way with a pertinent story, the salespeople in the audience can identify with that situation.

Wit is the sudden marriage of ideas which before their marriage were not perceived to have any relationship.   —Mark Twain

Laughter is inner jogging.
—Norman Cousins

A good sense of humor makes for good *business*...Doing business is a human activity, and a sense of humor is an essential ingredient of our humanity. The unrelievedly serious face quickly becomes a corporate liability. Put another way: humor is cost effective. It helps a company be more productive, and it goes far in making the company more compassionate. Humor has always been one of our best national resources. In fact, I'd like to believe that our country's productivity, it's prosperity, its very progress as a nation, is related directly to our sense of humor, our easy adaptability, as a people. Humor is very practical, enormously powerful....

—Sanford S. Pinsker,
Associate Professor in Business Horizons,
Franklin & Marshall College

CHAPTER 15

Strategic Alliances—Making the Team Work

Sales managers are planners, leaders, and analyzers. They are rarely salespeople. Sales managers make alliances with individuals, departments, and companies that can further the team's goals. *Webster's* defines strategic alliances as "...a form of networking or brainstorming...through cooperative marketing...they cross-promote the interests of each member of the alliance." (Gustav Berle, *The Small Business Information Handbook,* John Wiley & Sons, 1990).

A sales manager's alliances or symbiotic relationships might include the following:

- Company top management
- Clerical staff (order processing and bookkeeping)
- Credit department
- Shipping department and warehouse staff
- Truckers and delivery crew
- Production or service department head
- Suppliers
- Marketing, advertising, and public relations personnel
- Trade and professional associations
- Independent sales representatives
- International trade specialists
- Customers, customers, customers
- Bankers, lenders, and leasing companies

- Government resources, where applicable
- The sales manager's family may be his or her closest ally

Strategic alliances can be built on limited, local relationships. All over the country, business consultants and sales representatives from different, usually non-competing, local companies meet weekly in a local hotel for brainstorming. Each member relates the kind of calls and sales successes he or she had during the past week. Then they exchange names of companies, contact persons, and the perceived needs of the business.

Eventually, every member of this "strategic alliance" club picks up a lead about a new business that has opened or a new owner or manager who has taken over. They also exchange "red flags" about companies that appear to be on the verge of failure or are slow pay. In addition, they trade business cards, which can be passed on to prospects if the opportunity presents itself.

Additional opportunities arise when they need goods and services. They are able to network with each other and, in some cases, buy products as a group at quantity discounts.

Strategic alliances operate on many levels and are not necessarily restricted to the province of the *Fortune* 500.

The Internal Sell

One of the most important strategic alliances, perhaps the most important, is the one you develop with the people in your own company. Few activities can demoralize you and your sales representatives more than conflicts within your own house.

From the sales manager's viewpoint, the sales effort could be crippled if other departments fail to understand the selling environment and are insensitive to the needs of the sales staff.

The following comments are typical of what is often voiced at sales meetings:

> The internal sale is the hardest.
>
> If I can get through to those scientific airheads with the white socks...
>
> If those blankety-blank MBAs in marketing had more experience and less schoolhouse theory...

Why do those people in credit insist on being the anti-sales department?

At the same time, the marketing, R&D, credit, personnel, and production departments look at the sales department and vent their frustrations by asking:

Why can't those sales turkeys get their act together?

How come those sales guys are not more responsive to *our* needs?

Willie Loman is alive and well in our sales department

If the sales department could forecast, we would be able to get out enough goods when the *customer* wants them.

This kind of bickering goes on in most companies. It is a lose–lose situation and needs to be neutralized. An aura of misunderstanding and distrust leads to lost sales and shrinking profits.

To resolve the conflict, plan to get all the salespeople together. If yours is a big company, bring the district sales managers together for a hands-on, let-your-hair-down get-together. With management's approval, invite representatives from all other internal departments to attend. The following should be considered:

- Marketing
- Product management
- Customer service
- Technical service
- Credit and collections
- Research and development
- Manufacturing
- Purchasing

Prepare your presentation carefully from the viewpoint of the various company levels:

- Top management
- District managers
- Other department managers
- Sales representatives

It will be up to you to represent or have someone from the marketing department represent the most important person of all: the customer.

It is important at such an internal strategic alliance meeting to spotlight each department's comments, objections, and contributions. A large flip chart is a good tool.

Airing your department's needs and expectations enlightens everyone. Getting other departments to open up and present their views makes them feel part of the greater team. Flip-chart sheets can be placed around the room so that each situation, proposal, problem, and solution can be seen clearly and compared.

A memo that capsulizes all ideas and solutions can be prepared the following day and sent to all participants. Everyone will gain a better appreciation of the sales division's role and understand how each department's activities contribute to reaching the company's goals and satisfing the customer.

This is the ultimate team-building exercise. Such a meeting of the minds can help increase sales and profits and reduce stress and tensions.

Your Best Ally: Your Customer

Of all the strategic alliances, the one you forge with the customer is key. This alliance is not limited to the sales department's contact with the customer. Other departments within your company also come in contact with the customer you have been trying so diligently to attract and keep. This emphasizes the need for the sales team-building exercise just discussed. *Everyone,* not just sales personnel, is involved in the customer-retention process.

One successful Illinois business services company takes customer strategic alliances very seriously. Every employee gets a spiralbound book entitled *The Customer: Handle with Care.* The policy is reinforced with reminders from the president and others, and instructional videos are used at the frequent employee meetings. This company makes sure that every staff member who comes in contact with a customer knows the importance of a customer strategic alliance.

The company's training director says, "We let [our employees] know that the customer is our lifeblood, because without our customers, we wouldn't be around. And we tell them how much more profitable we are with a good customer base, rather than the more expensive price of finding new customers. As [the president] often points out, it is much less expensive to retain a customer than to find a new one."

A recent note in both *Entrepreneur* and *INC.* magazines emphasized that it costs about five times as much to attract a new customer as to retain an existing one. It is a dramatic point that needs to be made to your salespeople daily.

Strategic Alliances Are Everywhere

Establishing the kind of contacts that can lead to sales and retain customers goes well beyond the sales department. However, we need to look at the big picture. The efforts of other departments support the top of the pyramid. Without the final marketing effort—the sale—nothing much happens.

Our efforts can whither on the vine if someone down the line in distribution or production screws up. We need to be aware of the overall picture, because it is in our self-interest to do so. As John Donne said several centuries ago: "No man is an island."

One important strategic alliance is with a larger company, even a competitor. Today, many large companies are reducing their operations to a more manageable size. They have found that some functions can efficiently and economically be subcontracted to smaller, more flexible companies.

It has become commonplace to farm out everything from R&D to manufacturing specialized components to providing local/regional services. Big companies, instead of banks, often subsidize smaller companies, building mutually beneficial strategic alliances or symbiotic arrangements. Such alliances often earn not only a company's gratitude but a very large customer.

The Japanese take building alliances very seriously. Their sales and marketing people explore and forge such alliances, and their production and R&D managers travel around the globe to forge alliances that will enhance sales. Regis McKenna, a California marketing consultant, said that "you have to have a sense throughout the organization that the building of relationships is everybody's job, even if you never see a customer."

He cites the classic story of Henry Ford, who said that the customer can get any automobile he wants, as long as it is black. Ford was outsold by General Motors, which gave customers *choices*. McKenna also points to other support people: "Manufacturing people have to produce high-quality, low-cost products on time. If you're a shipping clerk, you make sure that the right things are in the container, that the directions are there. Telephone operators, too, have to be in touch with the marketplace."

Ours will continue to be a customer-driven marketplace and service, service, service is the byword.

Don't Forget Your Salespeople!—Making the Team Work

National Hockey League star Wayne Gretzky says, "The best players in hockey are the ones who make their teammates look good, the ones who make their teams win. If there is one thing I'd like to be remembered for, it's that I tried to think of 'them' more than 'me.'"

Do you need to form a strategic alliance with your own salespeople? Absolutely. Without their cooperation and loyalty, you are operating in a vacuum. According to the accumulated wisdom of well-known, super-successful executives like Robert "We Try Harder" Townsend:

- 20 percent of any given group of salespeople will usually produce 80 percent of the sales. Determine who is in this top group and focus on them. Give them what they need, and they will produce even more.

- Compensation should increase in proportion to a salesperson's achievement. An example of a good compensation incentive would be 5 percent on the first $100,000, 7.5 percent on the next $100,000, and so forth. Don't modify this incentive scale if the salesperson earns a fortune, because you will, too.

- Top sales producers should be offered stock options and encouraged to think like owners.

- If salespeople produce in superior fashion, keep them producing what they obviously enjoy and are good at. Don't pull them out of their nirvana and make them district sales managers or managers at headquarters. A salesperson is one breed, and a manager is another. "Most good salespeople thrive in the field, wither at headquarters," writes Robert Townsend.

Alliances to Avoid

Not all strategic alliances are worthwhile. Two that come to mind are *raiding* and *nepotism*. Sometimes you can't avoid getting caught up in them, but if you can, it is in your best interest to do so.

Raiding other companies for their best sales producers might sound like an easy way to acquire top-notch talent. But consider the implications carefully. If people who are willing to jump ship for a few extra bucks become unhappy on your turf, they will do the same to you if money, prestige, recognition, etc. do not come quickly enough. And chances are they won't. It takes time to realign and develop contacts and new alliances. The euphoria of a new company relationship evaporates quickly if it takes too long to see the rewards.

When you poach from other companies—especially competitors— you usually get someone who is dissatisfied with his or her current relationship. That same person might, usually within a year, find that the new company is no nirvana either, and performance will reflect this attitude. If you're lucky, another competitor will steal the person away and solve your problem.

Sometimes you can get caught in the middle of nepotism. How do you handle the incompetent brother-in-law of the company's president? He takes up space, preempts a territory that somebody else could make productive, creates dissatisfaction among the rest of the crew, and is a demoralizing role model. But you are stuck with the problem.

It could be worse if you own the company and the brother-in-law is related to your spouse. The irreverent Robert Townsend says: "Nepotism is a way of screwing the non-family shareholders. If all the shareholders are family, then it doesn't matter; they're only screwing each other. But when Ford Motor Company stock was sold to the public, Henry II and his brothers should have gotten out of the management. When they didn't, it seemed inevitable that their first classic misadventure should turn out to be named after a relative."

The tragedy is that the really good people, once they smell nepotism, will avoid going to work for you in the first place.

It is important to establish and maintain sound strategic alliances with international trade specialists if foreign sales are part of your portfolio. This is a horse of a very different color, and the next chapter is devoted to selling overseas.

If selling to the U.S. government—the world's biggest customer—is your responsibility, alliances here are very special. Unless you have previous experience in this field, you need to study the idiosyncrasies of this type of alliance.

A number of books detail the techniques, caveats, and rules that generally apply to both federal and state purchasing methods. They all say one thing in common: Government purchasing regulations, including forms and red tape, need to be followed to the letter. Any deviation from procedures, specifications, dates, or pricing will assure that your sales proposal will be rejected. Each department usually has bureaucrats who earn their salary trying to be helpful.

Each government purchasing department has a special minority assistance section, and there are also outside government and quasi-government agencies that can help you in the selling process. All assistance is free and confidential. The Small Business Administration can be especially helpful if you can find the right contact within the agency's 105 field offices, hundreds of affiliated SBDC (Small Business Development Centers), or SCORE (Service Corps of Retired Executives) offices. The help is free.

Dealing with the government requires:

1.   Patience, patience, and more patience
2.   Strict adherence to established regulations and procedures

If you can hack these, then you could develop a valuable strategic alliance with a multi-billion-dollar customer.

CHAPTER 16

Selling Overseas—The Impact of Export

More than 20,000 small American companies are already engaged in international trade. Most larger companies are already trading with partners abroad or are at least considering it. In many cases, international trade has proven very profitable, despite the obstacles and pitfalls.

The U.S. deficit in international trade shows that the American market demands foreign goods and has the means to pay for them. Led by oil imports and foreign cars, the U.S. international trade balance has been quite lopsided for years. No wonder, then, that several agencies of the federal government and virtually every state have departments that aid and encourage domestic companies to seek greater export volume.

Every state has an overseas trade office available to help explore trading possibilities. In Washington, D.C., the Department of Commerce and the Small Business Administration, and their various subsidiary agencies, have well-developed programs that provide literature, counseling, trade fairs, product/service want ads, and even financing to encourage export.

When forming sales plans for your company, thousands of private export/import management companies, banks with international expertise and overseas connections, chambers of commerce, international trade associations, and universities with courses in international trade can be of inestimable help.

One concern about trading overseas is financing the operation. Again, many banks and government programs can bridge the difficulties of money transfers and ensure that American sellers receive just compensation. A letter of credit, especially one that can be confirmed by a U.S. bank, or advance payment by the purchaser is the preferred way of dealing abroad. In some cases, a barter arrangement is the only way a deal can be made in currencies that have uncertain U.S. exchange value.

Sales managers and companies that are used to dealing only with domestic companies know that receivables take an average of 42 days to collect. It is more difficult to collect foreign receivables, unless advance payment or a confirmed letter of credit has been negotiated ahead of shipment.

Conditions abroad change constantly, and sales or export managers must keep abreast of political and economic conditions. At the start of 1993, for instance, the following countries had significantly longer times periods compared to the 42-day average in the United States:

Country	Average Collection Days
Algeria	103
Morocco	105
Cameroon	106
Ecuador	107
Chile	109
Tunisia	116
Uruguay	120
Argentina	121
Ethiopia	138
Kenya	143
Syria	175
Iran	310

The lengthy payback period is just one problem. Another is the bad-debt ratio. In the United States, 1 percent is typically written off as bad debts or uncollectibles. Many domestic companies have experienced a 5 percent write-off when dealing with European companies. Naturally, this risk has to be factored into the product price. However, that is not the end of the story. If bad debts have to be collected through overseas courts, the variance in local laws and the need to hire local attorneys often prove to be more expensive than the cost of the goods or services sold in the first place.

The answer is not to avoid international trade, but to adapt to the different conditions. The smart-money international traders are converting foreign sales agents into foreign affiliates who will make sales and collect receivable—or share the losses. The existence of a domestic legal presence in "problem" foreign countries also has a psychological effect, which may make it easier to pursue and collect overdue accounts.

Preliminary Steps Prior to Selling Overseas

American companies and their sales managers can take the following preliminary steps:

- **Your company's capabilities**—Analyze your company's capabilities to expand production or services to accommodate additional overseas sales.

- **Export potential**—Study the export potential to determine in what countries it would be best to sell. Examine the competition's quality and pricing and what changes might have to be made to make your product or service acceptable to these foreign markets.

- **Market details**—Get details from American trade and government sources, as well as from the foreign countries' commercial offices, to make sure those markets are right for your product or service.

- **Product demand and profitability**—Study demand for shipment and sale into those countries, warehousing, distribution, money transfer, and any other special procedures that will make profitable trade feasible.

- **Export management company**—If your company is not set up to handle all these details, find an export management company to handle them on a fee or percentage basis.

- **The process**—Learn how the export process works from others. Seek advice from MBA students at universities who may work as consultants on exporting. Some consulting firms will give free advice the first time around.

Strategic Alliances Abroad

Just as sales management establishes relationships with local resources, setting up symbiotic arrangements with overseas warehouses, agents, distributors, and governments is crucial. The Japanese are masters of this technique.

Whether the product is autos, copiers, cameras, or computers, Japanese success in the United States is largely due to alliances with American entrepreneurs. Japanese manufacturers progressed rapidly in the United States because they linked their products and fortunes with thousands of independent U.S. dealers and distributors. Venture capital followed Japanese products, so that money boosted overseas profits.

Sam Kusumoto, chairman and CEO of the Minolta Corporation, which maintains American headquarters in Ramsey, New Jersey, stated, "Frankly speaking, without our independent dealers, Minolta would be nothing in this country."

Ambassador Hiromoto Seki, Consul General of Japan in New York, admitted that "it's part of our partnership...national boundaries are rapidly being replaced by international alliances and affinities." He noted that "the average Japanese young man, for example, spends a typical day by waking up to the music of Madonna, shaving with a Gillette razor, having breakfast at McDonald's, talking with customers on a Motorola cellular telephone, and chatting over Pepsi Cola and popcorn."

Eyeing the North American market, the long-range-oriented Japanese manufacturers saw a region far too large to do business effectively on their own. The solution was to establish creative product distribution and research and service channels in cooperation with individual U.S. entrepreneurs.

It is a technique that American sales managers might well consider. Just as in domestic situations, it involves the following steps:

1. Investigate and research the market thoroughly.
2. Adapt products and services to the market.
3. Form alliances with domestic distributors.
4. Take a long-term view to achieve commercial success

How to Sell Overseas Like a Native

The stereotypical (often called "ugly") American tourist has given Yankee salesmen a bad reputation. American entrepreneur Wilson Harrell spent ten years in Europe making his sales successes, punctuated by a lot of admitted failures. He warns that people in foreign lands march to a different drummer, even though they like American music.

To Europeans, an entrepreneur is an oddity. Harrell opines that we look like Americans and speaking English just confuses them more. "We are an unknown breed. We know little or nothing about them or their culture and won't take time to learn. We are strangers, and in most languages, 'stranger' and 'enemy' are the same word."

Harrell is justifiably a bit pessimistic about your initial reception. He advises patience above all. "Negotiation is an art form...Don't plan to visit 10 countries in 10 days and close 10 deals. Go to one country with an open return ticket. Make sure it's *you* who says, 'let's think this over overnight!' "

Harrell also suggests using caution if the overseas representative from the United States is a woman. "Most foreigners simply do not know what to do with women." He claims to have been the first American to use a female rep abroad. She was so successful that she was able to start a chain of gift stores with her own money.

As a final bit of advice, Wilson Harrell suggests using a big international accounting firm that has offices in the country in which you are doing business. The local partners have in-depth studies of markets and consumers, as well as the executives you need to meet.

The following books and publications, some available free or at low cost from the U.S. Department of Commerce's International Trade section and revised periodically, may be helpful:

- *Do's and Taboos Around the World* (3rd edition), by Roger E. Axtell (John Wiley & Sons)
- "Exporter's Guide to Federal Resources for Small Business," Small Business Administration or U.S. Government Printing Office, Washington D.C. 20402
- *Business Information Sourcebok,* by Gustav Berle (Wiley)—listings of books, periodicals, directories, and government resources
- *Exportise, An International Trade Source Book,* The Small Business Foundation of America, 20 Park Plaza, Boston, MA 02116

Establishing Your Overseas Sales Force

One or a combination of methods can help to sell your products and services overseas:

1. Direct sales through your own efforts
2. International trade fairs

3. Agents and distributors already established overseas
4. Professional Export Management Companies (EMCs)
5. Such marketing tools as foreign trade zones
6. Agents indigenous to a particular country
7. If large enough, use of your own offices in strategic overseas locations (especially those where the United States or your state might already have a trade representative)

Direct sales are obviously difficult and expensive, unless you have a large volume of business, lots of experience, and very good contacts. It is unlikely that you will be able to march into a foreign country and establish your own sales force or send a rep from the United States unless that person is a former native of that country and experienced in its way of doing business. In some countries, you will not be able to get a license to trade there unless you are represented by or in partnership with a citizen of that country.

International trade fairs and leasing of storage facilities can be made easier and more economical, especially for smaller exporters, if the American international trader joins others in a kind of trade association or group. Several manufacturers/suppliers can generate sufficient sales to make a full container load feasible, lease warehouse space together, and be represented at costly trade fairs as a group rather than as individuals.

A decade ago, some Florida nursery owners got together to take advantage of European demand for interior plantings. They worked out an operating method, were able to buy bottom-rate full-container freight and one overall insurance policy, purchased economical transit storage in the Netherlands, and jointly attended at a major trade fair in Dusseldorf, Germany. This symbiotic arrangement proved to be effective and profitable for all members.

If you are considering direct selling overseas, consider the following four questions:

1. Is marketing in the foreign country available? For example, is advertising uniformly effective where it is available?
2. Have you studied cultural differences? They can have a dramatic effect on your sales and marketing approach.
3. Trade shows and fairs are great in some places, but would they be effective in the country where you are contemplating a sales effort?

4. The metric system could affect your product, or at least its documentation. Have you complied with the measurements, instructions, and so forth in the foreign country?

One innovative marketer in the Mediterranean area, unable to find adequate representation and outlets, organized a floating trade fair aboard a converted ship. He sold space to numerous exhibitors, arranged to sail to various port cities, and brought prospects and customers to them without the necessity of a local sales force.

Agents and distributors are the most common forms of overseas representation. Agents sell for you on a commission basis, and you handle shipping, credit, and collections. Distributors import your product and pay you for the merchandise. They then resell at a profit to their customers and make their own collections.

Agents are more commonly used for capital equipment, aircraft, military goods, and plant installations. Since they handle big transactions, their deals can take years to bear fruit. They are high-caliber business people whose reputation, connections, and experience with governments or major industries are their stock-in-trade.

Another use of agents is for high-volume, low-priced consumer goods, as found in chain stores. Since agents sell direct, usually at a commission of 10 to 15 percent, they can be highly competitive compared to local distributors buying from exporters—whose markup might be 50 to 70 percent.

The advantage of using distributors is that they inventory your products in foreign warehouses. They can deliver products quickly, usually have their own sales force in place, and assume all the cost for sales, credit, and collections. It is important that you establish price parameters with your overseas distributor, if this is the way you plan to operate, in order to remain competitive and assure repeat sales.

You need to consider the following points in your distributor agreement:

- Products that can be distributed
- Channels of distribution
- Specific authorized territories
- Inventory to be maintained
- Minimum amount of sales over a specific period
- Price and currency fluctuation

Export Management Companies (EMCs) are ideal agents for smaller American companies that want to explore overseas sales. There are fewer than 1,000 EMCs in the United States, and they range from one-person offices to highly sophisticated and specialized corporations. Because EMCs are domestic firms, you sell to them just as you would to any other American company.

These agents work on discounts taken at the time of sale, and you need to know little about the details and paperwork entailed in international trade. Payment terms depend on the size and liquidity of the EMC but are usually 10 to 20 percent below your best domestic price. The EMC marks up your goods another 30 to 40 percent in order to cover the services and risks involved in reselling overseas.

While the educational and selling advantages of hiring an EMC are evident, there are also some drawbacks. They depend on the seriousness of your entry into the overseas market, your long-range intentions, and your control of the market.

Selling through EMCs is less profitable and less risky, and you don't always have control over the type of merchandise the EMC favors at any given time.

Local ITA (International Trade Agency of the U.S. Department of Commerce) and Small Business Administration offices can be useful in finding and setting up the right EMC relationship. See also the previously mentioned sources, exporting trade journals, or contact the National Association of Export Companies, 17 Battery Place, New York, NY 10004.

Opportunities in the Future

One of the puzzles in international trade is the kind of doublethink practiced in Washington. Constituents often put pressure on their congressional representatives to establish protective export barriers. Yet the very same protesters buy machinery abroad because it is either better or cheaper.

Protective tariffs are counterproductive. They make the American consumer pay more for goods, reduce competitiveness, and sometimes even reduce the quality of goods offered.

Globally, U.S. exports have nearly doubled since 1985, from $219 billion to $422 billion. The huge U.S. deficit is due primarily to automobiles and oil. The near doubling of exports has in turn created millions of new jobs in the United States or at least has allowed jobs lost to foreign imports to be converted into exportable goods manufacturing.

The United States has grown to be the biggest exporter; it has passed Germany and certainly Japan, which is now in third place. Having a deficit with one country, such as Japan, does not mean that we have "lost" so many billions of dollars. Trade today is global. For example, suppose the United States sells $5 billion worth of goods to Japan and buys $5 billion worth of electronic and automotive products, and Japan in turn buys $5 billion of raw materials from the Chinese Republic, which is then able to buy $5 billion of U.S. wheat. The bottom line a deficit with one country and a positive balance with another. The example may be a simplification, but that's what makes world trade go 'round.

The American company that is innovative and has marketing savvy— and marketing is what Americans are best known for abroad—will recognize global trade opportunities and profit from them in the coming decade.

Coca-Cola and Schick, as well as McDonald's and other fast-food companies, offer proof that our arch-competitors, the Japanese, are indeed receptive to American products. Today, a U.S. consumer purchases an average of $357 in Japanese goods annually; the Japanese consumer, on the other hand, buys an average of $372 of made-in-the-USA merchandise every year.

In Japan, which at the time of this writing has somewhat stronger protective tariffs than the United States does, a young man in Tokyo who wants a pair of genuine Wrangler jeans pays $53.63. His counterpart in an American city pays $29.95 to $32. When the Japanese young man needs a new spark plug for his Toyota, he has to shell out $7.60. The American can go to an automotive supply department or store and get one for $1.69.

Technological advances in the world of business have made it feasible for a sales manager to deal overseas without ever leaving our shores. Foreign buyers love to come to the United States. You can meet many of them at international airport lounges or international trade fairs in Miami, San Francisco, or New York.

Federal and state agencies grind out tons of information that you can react to right at your desk. Visit the foreign service officers at consulates and embassies and make friends with them. They can be great sources of trade leads for products needed in their countries. If you already have distributors overseas, stay in touch with them regularly by phone, fax, or letter, and they will respond in kind.

If you do have to go overseas and you don't know your way around or speak the language, hire a taxi driver and a competent translator. The cost will pay for itself in time saved. If language is a problem, even at home, remember that the AT&T Language Line provides expert translation services in 140 languages.

Wilson Harrell provides a concluding thought: "The worst weapon an entrepreneur takes abroad is the ability to make decisions. Take it easy. When in Rome, do as the Romans do. Study the people, the geography, the customs, learn how to say merci, danke, taxameka, dekuij, efcharisto, gracias, spacibo. It all means the same: thank you. Chances are that it will be one word more than your competitor has been able to learn."

CHAPTER 17

Environment, Ethics, and Quality

The environment must come first. It has been around for a few billion years, or at least a couple of million since *Homo erectus* became *Homo sapiens*. Ironically, it took about five billion years to foul up the earth to such a degree that we have begun to notice that something is amiss.

People have become seriously concerned about the environment. The air we breathe, the water we drink, the sun we draw life from, and ground in which we grow things are all becoming precious commodities and endangered species. A score of years ago, Pogo, the comic strip muskrat created by Walt Kelly, announced: "I have met the enemy—and it is us!" One Canadian official recently pronounced that we have made the world into a garbage can and are living on the bottom of it.

From the sales management viewpoint, what is important is this: Millions of people in the industrialized world—our customers—have suddenly become aware of the degradation of the environment and are eager to reverse the destructive cycle, if it is not too late.

The March 1994 issue of *American Demographics* magazine reported that 55 percent of Americans actively engaged in some form of environmental activity in 1993. The article cited Roper Starch's "Green Gauge Study," which categorizes Americans into five groups based on their level of environmental productivity:

1. "True-Blue Greens" have made substantial changes in shopping behavior and personal habits.
2. "Greenback Greens" are pro-environment voters who contribute to environmental organizations.

3. "Sprouts" those who are beginning to accept environmental messages.

4. "Grousers" are the least active environmentalists.

5. "Basic Browns" are the most apathetic group.

Which level describes you and your company? Any company that can find a way to get on this "green" bandwagon of public concern has a tremendous advantage to offer its salespeople. "Green" entrepreneuring means not wasting irreplaceable resources, using biodegradable materials, and producing things from raw products that are not harmful to consumers. The *American Demographics* article cited the Roper Starch poll results which showed that consumers want businesses to educate them about environmentally sound products and what constitutes good and bad environmental practices.

Perhaps this concept, as well as the subsequent topic of ethics, and business appear to be an oxymoron, oil-and-water ideologies that do not mix. But the only contradictory action is the refusal to admit our mistakes and to look for solutions.

When your company does something that is good for the environment, gives the company a good image, appeals to consumers, and at the same time does not greatly increase product cost, you have an unbeatable market tool.

Energy companies of all stripes; clothing companies like Wrangler, Esprit, and The Baby Shop; automotive stations like Ecotech and Jiffylube; food companies like Ben & Jerry's and McDonald's; hotel giants like Marriott; and even financial institutions like Vermont National Bank, Dreyfus, Kemper, Fidelity, and Oppenheimer have seen the "green" light.

For example, early in 1994, Wrangler broke into a major nationwide retail account, largely as a result of the innovative environmental changes incorporated into its new "Earth Wash" jeans line. Like most of its direct competitors, the company is working to address the environmental concerns of its customers without hiking prices or sacrificing quality, comfort, look, or brand-name trust. Early sales have been encouraging.

If the public perceives your company or product to be a good citizen by helping to promote a healthier environment for everyone, the attention will show up on the corporate bottom line as profit.

Ethics

The rather sophisticated concept called *ethics* probably emerged around 3,400 or 3,500 years ago. A man named Moses, with a little help from a higher authority, developed the Ten Commandments.

These basic moral commitments started human beings on the long uphill climb toward ethical behavior. We are a long way from the top, and it is doubtful we will ever reach it. However, during the past century, we have made considerable strides, most often with the help of regulatory agencies and restrictive laws that curb our basic entrepreneurial instincts.

Since the era of the so-called "robber barons" over a hundred years ago, ethics has become a grudgingly accepted part of business. The Tylenol poisoning case caught pharmaceutical giant Johnson & Johnson flatfooted. But a company ethics policy had been written many decades earlier by founder General Wood Johnson. Had management executives not abided by this policy, Johnson & Johnson might be history. Instead, the company invested nearly $100 million and candidly discussed the problem with all of its customers. Its sales reps pulled all old stock off the shelves, and a new sealed package was developed (creating a whole new industry for America). Within a relatively short period, Tylenol again took its leadership position in the American marketplace.

Ethics, like the environment, is now the subject of innumerable business courses in colleges throughout the nation. These courses emphasize that highly sophisticated ethical concerns have a rightful place in corporate policy, and businesses that develop ethical policies invariably sport a better profit picture. They also have a healthy public relations image and are highly regarded by employees, suppliers, and customers.

Accepting ethics and environmental concerns as part of our business life is not always easy. A small business just getting off the ground might be hard-pressed to make a decision in favor of ethics and the environment. Likewise, if sales reps are faced with a decision of either doing right by the customer or making a higher commission, one's self-interest usually comes first.

It would be difficult to train salespeople to be ethical if they were not already moral human beings. The only way such moral and social concerns can find their way into company operations is for management to be convinced that this is the way to do business. Such a policy can be implemented and will likely show up as a sound bottom line only when top management:

1. Promulgates a policy of ethics in business
2. Continues to practice and teach it
3. Makes sure that every employee understands and subscribes to such company policy
4. Is convinced that such a policy is in *everyone's* best interest

Quality

Quality is the other ingredient in this triad of service. Practicing quality production and service on every level has been a byword for the last score of years. The ideas have been dramatized in several ways.

Phil Crosby has lectured and written books on the subject of quality control and its advantages. His Quality College in Winter Park, Florida, has been the training ground for thousands of corporation-sponsored managers who carried the Crosby Credo back to their home offices and companies. Another recent popular book said: "If you cannot do it right the first time, will you have time to do it over again?"

One reason U.S. citizens accepted Japanese automobiles is that these cars were thought to be better quality. Repeatedly, surveys have indicated that the repair records of Japanese cars are better than those for domestic cars.

Japanese, German, and Swedish automobile workers are no better qualified than their American counterparts; therefore, the cars are not superior for that reason. We can do as well or better if we have top management's commitment to give American workers quality training and motivation. It starts at the top and works its way through the management ranks to the workers.

Sound motivation techniques also encourage superior job performance at the sales level. With the right motivation to produce at a top quality level, personal productivity is increased, employee turnover is reduced, and the quality and level of sales and service are increased.

High-quality products and services mean that the customer will probably return again and again. Given that it costs a company five times as much to get a new customer as to retain an existing one, quality service wins hands down.

Social scientists have long preached that money and fringe benefits alone are not enough to create a quality sales and production climate. Effective management direction, motivated employees, and continuous follow-up are mandatory ingredients for a successful quality production and sales team.

Once quality and pride of workmanship are established, productivity and profitability will become natural by-products. These conclusions are by no means natural; they need to be taught—over and over again—to all employees on all levels. Quality training and quality performance imply continuity in effort on both sides.

Optimum results can be expected from a quality sales force if strict attention is paid to nine important factors:

1. Building and preserving a good quality reputation among customers

2. Retaining existing customers using available means

3. Quality management acting as a role model

4. Providing quality training without skimping

5. Acquiring quality new accounts to avoid future disappointments and credit crunches

6. Setting realistic sales targets and meeting them

7. Acquiring knowledge of products and technical information through continuous training

8. Continuously monitoring the frequency of sales calls and coverage of territory by sales management

9. Encouraging innovativeness, within the boundaries of company policy, and encouraging reps' efforts and potentially valuable ideas

Pretty Good Is Not Good Enough

A pretty good student sat in a pretty good class and was taught by a pretty good teacher, who always let pretty good pass. The pretty good student lived a pretty good town and graduated from a pretty good school only to find, when he started looking for a job, that "pretty good might not be good enough." Indeed, getting a job was tough. The moral is: "There once was a pretty good nation, pretty proud of the greatness it had, which learned, much to late, that if you want to be great, pretty good is, in fact, pretty bad."

When you boil it down to pretty good sales people and quality management training, what is critical to personal success? There are seven critical issues to consider when involving salespeople in quality training:

1. Offer salespeople a training program on how to close more sales, and they will probably show up.

2. Offer a training program on cold-call selling techniques, and few will attend.

3. Put one on about the company's latest total quality management initiative, and you'll likely spend a lonely afternoon staring at rows of chairs.

4. Salespeople can think of many better ways to occupy their time than sitting in a classroom (selling and making money, for example).

5. Fundamentally, there are lots of things that are more critical to the job and to their personal success than training.

6. This is especially true for training perceived as faddish or a program foisted upon them by the home office.

7. Many sales reps view total quality management training as an intrusion on their time. There is a tendency to view quality improvement as a set of bureaucratic procedures.

Five Steps for Selling Total Quality Management to Salespeople

As a sales manager, you will be involved in attracting your sales team to the company's total quality management (TQM) training programs, you will want to structure the curriculum so that it will appeal to your sales reps. To ensure that the training truly supports organization-wide quality, you need to:

1. **Integrate TQM into the sales process**—Avoid the perception that TQM is a "back office" initiative and only applies to researchers and manufacturing workers responsible for creating and producing products, or that it is just another "program of the month" imposed on the sales force and then abandoned. You must help with the front-end work. Use your understanding of the company's sales

culture to design customized programs. Off-the-shelf programs won't cut it.

2. **Leverage existing sales training to support TQM**—Quality training can fit well into existing sales training programs that emphasize identifying and satisfying customer requirements and expectations.

3. **Provide concrete sales examples**—Begin the quality training in terms your salespeople deal with every day. In *Reengineering the Corporation,* his recent best seller, Michael Hammer says: "It's a matter of helping them think in terms of those sales processes like customer engagement, customer acquisition, and customer intensification—all of which cut across organizational boundaries to achieve desired results. More specifically, the defects involved might include poor coordination between sales and billing or disconnects between the seller's shipping department and the buyer's warehouse system."

4. **Show how TQM can help build customer partnerships**—Consultative and relationship selling is all about partnership and is also the driving force behind TQM. Your training and coaching should emphasize skills that help your salespeople expand the relationship beyond buyer and seller to include the customer's suppliers and the customer's customer.

5. **Use technology as a unifying element**—In the hands of salespeople, TQM becomes a powerful tool for gathering volumes of information about customers. To be useful, that information needs to be carefully managed. Sophisticated computer and communication equipment should be used to collect, collate, analyze, and disseminate customer data. As discussed in more detail in Chapter 13, training salespeople to use this technology may be as important to a TQM effort as the TQM training itself.

Above all, *the customers are kings.* They are not people who disturb your day; they are the reason for your day. They have more choices today than ever before, and they pick the product or service that is the most reliable, has the fewest problems, and makes them the most money.

In the future, quality control, more than cost control, will control corporate survival. Companies that sincerely pursue a policy of quality will survive and grow. The others will likely not be around.

The "New" Forces for the Nineties and Beyond

A strange thing has happened on the way to the cash register. People have discovered the words *environment, ethics,* and *quality.* We are thus faced with that fact that these three components will undoubtedly be a part of our marketing plans, for two reasons:

1. The people we sell to demand it with increasing fervor.
2. Many companies have discovered that addressing the environment, ethics, and quality actually enhance their bottom line.

If our customers know that we are responsible corporate citizens, we can increase sales, our good image, and our earnings, especially when the going gets tough.

Ben & Jerry's Ice Cream, for example, found that these three factors helped the company grow and get great publicity for its products. Giant companies like Johnson & Johnson knew instinctively that honesty could help them survive disaster.

The following true story is about a modest-sized manufacturer near Des Moines, Iowa. He started manufacturing trailers six years ago. He followed all government and engineering requirements, but he did not follow his logic. He knew that under ideal conditions, his product would hold up as stated. But instead of putting 1,000 pounds into the trailers, as the manufacturer recommended, some customers overloaded them. Instead of pulling the trailers at a perfectly adequate 65 miles an hour, some customers went over 75 miles an hour. Naturally, a few of the trailers came loose from their couplings and caused serious accidents. The subsequent lawsuits almost put the manufacturer out of business. Had a bolt been one-eighth of an inch thicker, it might have held up under the unexpected abuse. Unfortunately, the manufacturer learned this after the accidents and lawsuits.

The manufacturer also learned that products cannot be made within the limits of acceptable standards. They have to perform even under the most abusive and difficult conditions. In today's litigious, quality- and environment-conscious era, we can do no less.

There is much talk about Japan and its rise to an industrial power-house. Japanese workers are not better than American workers, nor do they work harder; the difference is that Japanese management appreciates the awesome power of reliability, durability, and quality.

The Iowa trailer manufacturer made immediate corrections by replacing the inadequate bolts at a cost of $1,800 plus labor. He then used a heavier bolt, which would take the abuse of careless customers, in all future production. General Electric voluntarily recognized a design error and replaced thousands of compressors on its 1988 refrigerators. The corporate write-off was $450 million.

Sometimes such manufacturing tragedies can be turned into marketing opportunities, and all the aforementioned companies are still very much in business. They also called in their employees and asked them what they would do under the circumstances and how they could help to prevent such job-threatening situations in the future. The result was a boost in employee morale and increased quality production.

As we head into the third millennium, we are still struggling with this "new" baggage: environment, ethics, and quality. We are coming to recognize them, even grudgingly coming to accept them, as necessary. But practicing them on a daily basis is still difficult. One problem is that top management in some companies still has not accepted this triad as necessary. If the top people in an organization are not sold on them and do not practice them, teach them, and insist on them, then those in the middle might find little reason to adhere to them either.

We in sales management must assume the role of conduit of tomorrow's lifestyle. Promoting environmental consciousness, a return to ethical business conduct, and quality products and services can only help us.

That the environment needs help is almost beyond argument any more. Despite the fact that there are five billion people crowding the planet, and tens of thousands of new lives are added daily, we will continue and succeed. We must find solutions that do not increase the pollution and degradation caused by human beings. In these very problems lie untold opportunities.

Those of us who want to do profitable business today *and* tomorrow need to recognize the consumer trend toward environment, ethics, and quality.

If we understand these concerns, then we can incorporate them into our price structure, our sales presentations, and, most of all, our own conscience.

The Ten Commandments of Personal Business Ethics

1. I shall not lie or misrepresent the facts about business activities I conduct or direct.

2. I shall not blame others, whether my superior or my inferior, for my personal mistakes.

3. I shall not divulge personal or confidential information.

4. I shall not permit, knowingly commit, or fail to report evident violations of a law or regulation.

5. I shall not cover up for others or protect incompetents when they endanger themselves, their fellow workers, or the public.

6. I shall not condone or fail to report the misuse or theft of company property.

7. I shall not deliberately suppress complaints or grievances.

8. I shall not cover up or fail to report accidents or conditions that can lead to accidents and the endangerment of the health and safety of others.

9. I shall not ignore or violate commitments made to employees by my superiors and company.

10. I shall not smuggle ideas of those working under me as ideas of my own or steal the accomplishments of others.

INDEX